STREET
WARRIOR

MALCOLM PRICE WITH STEPHEN RICHARDS

STREET WARRIOR

THE TRUE STORY OF THE LEGENDARY
MALCOLM PRICE, BRITAIN'S HARDEST MAN

JOHN BLAKE

Published by John Blake Publishing Ltd,
3 Bramber Court, 2 Bramber Road,
London W14 9PB, England

www.blake.co.uk

First published in paperback in 2006

·ISBN 1 84454 299 8

British Library Cataloguing-in-Publication Data:

A catalogue record for this book is available from the British Library.

Design by www.envydesign.co.uk

Printed in Great Britain by Bookmarque Ltd, Croydon, Surrey

1 3 5 7 9 10 8 6 4 2

Papers used by John Blake Publishing are natural, recyclable products made
from wood grown in sustainable forests. The manufacturing processes conform
to the environmental regulations of the country of origin.

Every attempt has been made to contact the relevant copyright-holders,
but some were unobtainable. We would be grateful if the appropriate
people could contact us.

*For the special lady who managed to turn
my life around and put me on the straight and narrow ...
which hasn't been easy for her. Thank you.*

Malcolm Price is a legend in his own lifetime. Hailing from Merthyr Tydfil, South Wales, he has developed one of the most awesome reputations as hard man in the UK. Fortunately for his enemies, he has recently taken time out to actively pursue ornithology.

Stephen Richards, no-holds-barred investigative journalist and spokesman for the underworld, is a regular contributor of gangland news to numerous websites. He is the author of several successful true crime books, many of which have been serialised in the national press. Richards has his own management company, Crimebiz, representing infamous and notorious underworld figures. He is often sought out by production and film companies and has advised on *Panorama* and Trevor McDonald's *Tonight* to name a few. He is also involved in producing and directing crime documentaries and big-screen gangster movie scripts.

CONTENTS

FOREWORD

We used to finish work on the Saturday around 12 o'clock and we'd go to what we had called the McShifters Arms, now the Great Western, in Merthyr. We'd get tanked up on a Saturday afternoon, Price and me. This particular Saturday, he decided he wanted to arm-wrestle me – he did and he won.

I was determined to get one over on him. There was this young girl in the corner, so I said to her, 'We're going to have a kissing competition in a minute, Bev, Pricey and me. We're going to practise on you and you are going to be the judge. Whatever happens, I'm going to be the winner and I'll buy your beer all afternoon.'

So, the kissing competition started and it lasted quite a while. And, at the end of it, I was judged by Bev to be the winner. Poor old Pricey, the square-jawed blond, he couldn't believe that he was the loser and I don't think to this day that he knew that I bought Bev beer all afternoon so I could be the winner! There was no way he was going to win, no matter how good a kisser he was and it dented his manhood somewhat and evened the score for me losing at arm-wrestling.

Although Price lost the kissing competition, he still had his image intact, as he was always surrounded by a bevy of beautiful girls. I remember Price was living with one of his many girlfriends at that time; I went to call for him on a Christmas morning so we could go out for a seasonal drink.

I remember the exact words his girlfriend said, as she said them directly to me: 'Now I'm warning you, if you don't get him back here by two o'clock for his Christmas dinner, this goose that he nagged me for, for weeks and weeks, goes in the bin!'

I said, 'I'll get him back in time.'

Out we went and Price had two, three, four, five and I'm looking at my watch now and it's ten minutes to two and I had promised to get Price back by two or his goose would be well and truly cooked, in more ways than one!

I said, 'Price, we've gotta make a move now.'

He was well over the top! He just pushed me out of the way, 'Don't tell me what to do.' I could tell he was turning then so I left him.

I went back up to the house to tell his girlfriend that Price wouldn't be there for Christmas dinner and, with that, she threw the goose straight into the bin like she had promised! A fully cooked goose straight in the bin!

That Christmas day, I last saw him when I left him in the pub just before two o'clock, and that very Christmas night he got locked up. He went from the Express pub to a pub called the Morlais Tavern. Price, tanked up, rolled into the pub at about seven or eight o'clock in the evening and there was this English chap there, sitting on a high stool by the bar. He didn't know Pricey. When Pricey got to the bar, he fell up against this English bloke who was none the wiser about who Price was.

The bloke told him where to get off; Price whacked him and headbutted him straight away and the landlord called the police. Price, as well as not getting his cooked goose, was locked up on Christmas night!

That wasn't the end of the story. She, his girlfriend, had had enough and left Price and went to stay with her mother. By the following week, she was still there and wouldn't go back to Price. Out of anger, he went round to her mother's house with an airgun and shot all of the windows out! They didn't get back together after that.

We were in the Express pub one night; we were in there until about three or four in the morning. We came out, and Price jumped straight into the car and he gave three of us a lift. There was no breathalyser back then so no one worried whether they'd had too much to drink. Down the road we went and Price drove straight into a lamppost and knocked the bumper off the car, which was hanging on by a thread and dragging along the road, sending a shower of sparks up into the air.

I said, 'Price, let's get out and pull it off and chuck it away.'

'Oh, bollocks! Fuck it, we'll keep going,' Price said.

So there we were going up the High Street with the bumper dragging alongside us, sparks were flying everywhere and there was this copper in the middle of the road waving his lit torch about wanting Price to stop!

Did Pricey stop? Did he hell! Straight around the copper and away he goes with the bumper still dragging along. He got away with that as well.

The amount of stories still going around about Pricey is nobody's business and they just make it up about him as they go along, but I have worked with him and was a drinking pal of his for many years. A lot of these stories people invent are derogatory, but what I am saying here is true.

As much as stories are going around about Price, it was the same with another Merthyr hard man. This man had an equally colourful reputation as Price, but was around long before Price came along. This man was called Redmond Coleman and he was around in the early 1900s. He was a bare-knuckle fighter and stories were still going around about him well into the 1960s.

As much as Price is a hard man, equally so, he is also an honest man. Price and I have been in all sorts of scrapes together and he and I might have gone into a shop on the way to work somewhere and, perhaps, the owner of the shop had to pop somewhere else and had left the shop unattended, which in certain parts of Wales was common, and I'd say to Price, 'Look at all the fags there we could have!' And, you know what? He wouldn't touch anything that didn't belong to him – that's how honest he was. He wouldn't pinch a pound if it was lying on the floor – he'd rather find out who owned it and hand it to them. If he even suspected that something was stolen then he wouldn't have anything to do with it.

I don't know if he had this honest streak bashed into him as a child, but, even though Price was physically bashed about by his old man, if his old man said to Price that he was getting abuse from so-and-so, then Price would go around and sort it out. That's just the way he was, a very selfless person who would always be giving himself to others. I think that right to the very end Price was still trying to get into his father's good books. He didn't disown his father, even though he had a difficult time at his father's hand.

Price wouldn't disrespect his father; he'd still call his old man 'Pops' right up until the end. All that his father had done to him didn't seem to dissuade Price from what he did for his father. For him, blood was thicker than water. His father didn't deserve to have him.

My wife's cousin lived next door to the Price family and his story was that Price's father, Les, would kick Malcolm around the room like a football! Nobody dared interfere. Les Price was almost as hard as Malcolm was when he was young.

I worked with Les as well, and everyone at work was afraid because Les was a bully. While Malcolm wasn't a bully, he was very aggressive. But Les was a bully even when he was sober; he would bully young kids and young men up on the opencast site where we worked, so everybody would be shit-scared of him. Malcolm was never like that, though. He was only aggressive when he was drunk.

There's no doubt that people used Malcolm for their own gain. I don't want to name names, but he had lots of hangers on. I think people who had a bit of a feud going on with someone else would sort of drag Price into their company so that they could use him if need be.

We were in the Horse and Groom pub one day – we called that the McShifters Arms as well. Whatever pub us earthmoving boys congregated in, we would christen it the McShifters Arms. We were in there one day and Price's best friend, Mike Mahoney, was in there. Now Mike was dressed immaculately – he always dressed like that. He always looked like a million dollars. He was already in there well before Price was, and this fellow, who I'll call Joe Bloggs came in, and he didn't like Mahoney.

Joe Bloggs said to Mahoney, 'I never liked you, Michael. I want to fight you.'

The bloke was drunk and Mahoney said to him, 'Leave it alone, I'm not bothered.'

This chap then pulled a £20 note out of his pocket and put it on the bar top and put his pint glass on top of it. He said to Mahoney, 'There you are, put your £20 there with it and when I come back from the toilet we'll fight for the £40.'

So off he went to the toilet. When Joe Bloggs was in the toilet, who should come into the bar but the man himself, Price.

Mahoney said to Price, 'Look at that £20 note underneath Joe Bloggs's glass.'

Price said, 'What's it there for?'

'Oh, he wants to fight me for it,' said Mahoney.

Price picks up the pint glass, puts the £20 in his pocket, winks at Mahoney, goes to the toilets and kicks the door open where Joe Bloggs was sitting having a crap. Joe looks up from where he was sitting and all he saw was a bunch of fives landing right between his eyes. And Price got to keep the £20.

Another time, we'd finished one of the jobs we were on for Christmas and headed back for Merthyr on a Friday and the first stop was the Tydfil Arms, where Price was sweet on the landlady. We had a few pints and a few pints more and a couple off the top shelf as well and Price was chatting the landlady up all the time, but she had to go and serve the other punters.

The landlady went to serve this gypsy and, while she was serving him, he caught hold of one of her hands and started chatting her up. She tried to pull her hand away but he was having none of it. When Price saw this, it was like a red rag to a bull! Price marched up to the gypsy and whacked him. If I went to pull him off then I'd have it as well, mate or no mate. You don't stop him when he goes. So he gives this gypsy a whack and down he goes and the gypsy starts grabbing at Price so Price starts putting the boot in as well.

I heard, with my own ears, the gypsy say, 'Allright, Price, I've had enough!'

Price looked at him in shock disbelief and said to him, 'I'll tell you when you've fucking had enough,' and he gave him another half-dozen boots!

I remember, I went to pick Price up for work one morning, at about five or six o'clock, and he had just come in from his night out on the tiles! I said, 'What's the matter with your mouth?' There was blood all around his mouth, every tooth in his head was loose; they were all shaky and bleeding.

He could hardly speak and he was slurring. He managed to mumble to me that he'd crashed his car. He slurred, 'I've just wrapped the Mercedes around a lamppost.' He had this huge Mercedes car that was built like a tank.

I said, 'Where's the car now?' So we jumped into my car and went down the road. When we got to where the accident had happened, I couldn't believe my eyes! No man could have walked away from what I saw, the lamppost was embedded in the car right up to the dashboard and it had carved its way through the bonnet. This wasn't one of those flimsy modern lampposts either! If it was a small car, then he wouldn't be here now, his car and his build had saved Price's life. After that, off we went to work! If that had been me, I would have to have taken the day off, but that's how Price was.

One morning, after a bellyful of beer, Price comes in to work the worse for wear. When Price was like that, he used to always look for a stream and dip his head into it and he was all right for a bit then.

We had an Irishman working with us called Jimmy Egan. When he saw Price looking to dip his head in the stream, he said, 'No, no! Don't dip it there, Price. Come up here, there's a nice clean pool.'

Price had his head submerged in it and was having a

right good session of washing and putting his head under the water when Egan walked across to Price, picked him up and took him up the stream a bit further and there was this rotten sheep lying in the stream! Price had been dousing himself in the very water that was washing past this stinking rotten dead sheep that had been hanging about for months. Egan then let Price go and ran like hell!

Although Price was a feared hard man, he could still take a joke. But I remember this particular day when he was deadly serious after a man said the wrong thing! Price is a very patriotic man, which was proven one day when we went into the McShifters Arms (The Great Western) where there was this Englishman, a big strapping fellow, Benjy Kendrick.

He was from South Yorkshire way, but had been living in Wales a while and having a relationship with a Welsh girl, but he had just had a big barney with her and he was calling Welsh women 'bastard Welsh women!'

Next thing, Price growls, 'Hey, don't you talk like that; my mother's a Welsh woman!' And, God, he swung a real haymaker at Benjy and Benjy dodged out of the way and Price's arm went straight through a plasterboard wall to above his elbow! Price was struggling to get his arm out, which wasn't easy, due to his jacket catching on the rough edges of the plasterboard. It was a long bar and Benjy started running, hoping he'd get to the door before Price released his trapped arm. Luckily for Benjy, he got out of the door before Pricey got his arm out of the wall!

There were times when Price was so drunk that he couldn't talk coherently – he'd be slurring and you couldn't understand him. But, the minute a bit of bother came along, he was at it like it was second nature to him. I never ever saw him in any scrap where he wasn't pissed up anyway, and yet I never ever saw him lose.

Although he had a tough exterior, he was a man with a soft heart. When Price's mother died he was at his wits' end. I took him in the car and we went up to a little place called Hay-on-Wye (the book capital of the world) and we spent the whole day up there and he got well into these bird books and nature books which he's mad about and all of his troubles seemed to melt away. Had I taken him to the pub then, for certain, trouble would have started.

By now, Price's reputation was made and stories about him were flying about like confetti. I invited Price to my wedding, but my father found out about it and said that Price wasn't welcome because it would lower the tone of the celebration. I stood my ground and, come five o'clock on the day of the wedding, my father was singing Price's praises. My father had been caught up in the hype that was going around about Price, but he soon learned that this was all it was. Unless you gave him trouble he wouldn't give any to you: he never went looking for it.

This is the sort of man Price is: a very friendly guy who respects people for what they are and his respect for older people is beyond comprehension. But, when he put troublemakers down on the floor, they stayed down until he was finished and not before.

Gareth 'Jonah' Jones

INTRODUCTION

The role of anti-hero has often been attributed to Malcolm Price, begging the question, what is it that makes anti-heroes and underdogs such crowd pleasers?

Every so often, along comes a man who makes his mark on mankind. From the days when David won the battle against Goliath right up to the time when man first set foot on the moon, there have been heroes for us to hold aloft. Often, there are untold stories of such men and upon first hearing these tales of such godlike figures we stand in awe and, often, disbelief at their superhuman feats. Eventually, an acceptance of what they achieved sets in and the myth is accepted as legend. How such mythical stories came about is not usually questioned.

The heroic deeds of the dead can be awe-inspiring, and include such acts as those of the soldiers on the front-line trenches during the First and Second World Wars. How men risked their lives in order to save their mortally wounded mates from No Man's Land astounds us, yet we, who have never risked ourselves in such an heroic way, can take on the role of the hero by just reading or hearing about their feats.

But what about anti-heroes? Can they be just as enthralling to us as those who have completed a superhuman deed that benefits mankind? Do we want to take on that role and adopt the persona of a hated person? The norm is for us is to be inspired by the likes of Scott of the Antarctic, the feats of Hercules or stories of how Grace Darling risked her life so that others could be saved from certain death.

The scenario where the sprawling anti-hero gets his comeuppance and the champion walks off into the sunset with his arm around the prize, usually a woman, is a pleasing one. This media personification of what a hero is all about used to be common. Examining past events can confirm this convoluted outlook that sees the baddie being portrayed as some sort of evil manifestation sent to cause havoc by any means possible.

History stands in judgement against those select few that are perceived as being do-badders. The well-known story of how the Russian 'Mad Monk', Rasputin, was up to no good soon changed when some filmmakers portrayed him as the one on the receiving end of others' evil actions.

Stalin, the Russian dictator, was, reputedly, responsible for the deaths of twenty million Russians, yet he is still held aloft by his fellow countrymen as the creator of something good. People, to this day, still put roses on Stalin's tomb.

The Welsh-made film *Twin Town* never received critical acclaim, but such lack of accolades gives it the cult status of never having quite made it due to always being in the shadows of the Scottish film *Trainspotting*. Two films that portrayed the anti-heroes as heroes! Sadly, Twin Town did not put Wales on the filmmaker's map.

The anti-hero has played an important role in the history of mankind, so much so that the whole ethos of what is good and bad has become blurred. Examining the background of anyone can bring skeletons to our attention; a blot on the landscape can mar all that pleases the eye. This is how Malcolm Price was perceived by those who would stand back in fear of what he was all about, yet there was much more to him than that.

To really know what Malcolm Price is all about we have to go back in time so as to be able to grasp the inherent values and behaviour instilled in him by virtue of his ancestral history. To be perceived as the hero, then the anti-hero and then the born-again hero needs some explaining.

Malcolm Price embodies all that is Welsh, aside from the green valleys and male voice choirs. The will to win against insurmountable odds is a penchant of the Welsh. Put this together with a propensity to never say 'die' and you begin to see what makes the Welsh so durable.

In the early 400s, Cunedda of the Gododdin settled in northwest Wales to defend the country against Irish attacks. Saxons were given permission to settle, as long as they helped fight off invasions by the Picts.

An army of Saxon 'hard men' was to see off attempts at a takeover, but by the late 400s the Saxons were starting to get a little too big for their boots and wanted to establish their own kingdoms within Britain. Along came a man by the name of King Arthur (Artorius Rex), and the Brythonic hero thwarted these Saxon attempts, if only for a short while!

In the 400s, Viroconium (Wroxeter, in Shropshire) was the capital of Powys. An inscribed stone dated to circa 480 was discovered in 1967, commemorating King Cunorix. Quite possibly, Arthur may have succeeded Cunorix, but Geoffrey of Monmouth says Arthur died in 537 at the Battle of Camlann.

The treacherous nephew of King Arthur, the evil Mordred (also called Maglocunus), was fabled to have killed Arthur in the battle at Camlann, so says Geoffrey of Monmouth. According to the Annales Cambriae records, it is said that both Arthur and Mordred fell at the battle.

The city of Viroconium was not abandoned until AD 520. There was no threat from the Anglo-Saxons for around 20 years, and Powys did not fall to the Anglo-Saxons until the 650s.

The Iron Town of Merthyr, in Wales, is the birthplace of Malcolm Price. Seeking to join present with past inspires a theory on the origins of King Arthur. This theory suggests that Arthur was king of Glamorgan and Gwent (Arthur ap Meurig ap Tewdrig). This person, it is said, was an early Christian centred on Caerleon and a string of hill forts. He died about AD 575, possibly at Merthyr Tydfil. His body was taken to the coast by ship to Ogmore up the River Ewenny and buried in a cave by the saint who, it was said, was Arthur's cousin. His body, legend has it, was left in a cave for some years so as to keep his death a secret until his son Morgan came of age.

By AD 650, most of England was under Saxon control, but that's as far as it went! The Saxon hopes for expansion were rendered impotent when it came to reaching out for glory beyond the Welsh mountains.

The territory of Wales was defined by a dyke, which stretched from sea to sea. In AD 780, the king of Mercia, Offa, ordered the construction of Offa's Dyke.

The territories of Wales were dispersed to the west of the dyke. Of these, Gwynedd (northwest Wales) was the most expansionist. The need to defend Wales from Viking attacks meant that some unity was needed.

Rhodri of Gwynedd (died AD 877) brought these kingdoms together and under his control, although it was his grandson Hywel (died AD 950) who finalised the unification process. In 1063, Harold, earl of Wessex, invaded Wales and Gruffudd was hunted down and killed.

The thirteenth century saw what was the most ambitious attempt to create a Welsh state. The rulers of Gwynedd paid homage to the king of England on behalf of the native rulers, and the lesser Welsh rulers paid homage to them. This policy was pursued by Llywelyn ap Iorwerth (died 1240), his son Dafydd ap Llywelyn (died 1246) and his grandson Llywelyn ap Gruffudd (died 1282). Their task was eased by the fact that the other major Welsh polities, Powys and Deheubarth, were, in the early thirteenth century, being divided into ever-smaller entities.

The principality of Wales, ruled by a Welsh dynasty, lasted from 1267 to 1282. Its first ten years were a period of hope, indicating that there were in medieval Wales all the elements necessary for the growth from factions to statehood.

Relations with the English crown deteriorated and, in 1276, the new king, Edward I, declared Llywelyn a rebel. Because of this, the prince was forced to submit. Through the Treaty of Aberconwy of 1277, he ceased to be overlord of most of the lesser Welsh rulers.

In the following five years, Llywelyn sought to consolidate his diminished principality, but, in 1282, his brother, Dafydd, rose in revolt, a revolt which Llywelyn eventually joined. This time, Edward was determined to achieve total victory. Llywelyn was killed near Builth on 11 December 1282 and Dafydd was executed at Shrewsbury in 1283.

Following Llywelyn's defeat, his principality was organised into six counties that were granted to the king's heir; thus the principality of Wales survived as an adjunct of the crown of England.

From the goings on just mentioned, it would be no surprise for you to learn that the people of Wales are descended from many ethnic groups, including the original Britons and other population groups including the Celts, Romans and Scandinavians. Around three-quarters of the present population of 2.94 million are concentrated around the large cities and mining valleys of the south-east of the country. In the last 100 years, Wales has welcomed many diverse new groups to settle and be part of its population, which is in direct contrast to the fierce defence of their borders that characterised Welsh history.

Had the fight been kicked out of the Welsh or was this about-turn connected to some ulterior motive? The two centuries after the conquest of Wales were a period of contradictory developments. Although there were no longer princely patrons, the poets flourished, with Dafydd ap Gwilym (died circa 1370) pre-eminent among them. Towns and trade developed, but the Black Death of 1349 cruelly reduced the population. Although most Welsh customs were unaffected by the conquest, the Welsh system of landholding was gradually undermined, and the estates of the gentry began to emerge.

Many Welshmen came to accept the conquest and large numbers of them served in the armies of the English kings. At the same time, there was resentment of English rule, which found expression in revolts in 1287, 1294 and 1316, and in serious disturbances in the 1340s and the 1370s. Above all, there was the great revolt of Owain Glyndwr (1400 – 10), which almost led to the re-establishment of Welsh rule.

A century after the Black Death, there were signs that the Welsh economy was recovering and economic growth occurred in the context of a ramshackle administrative system. The division between the principality and the March continued, and Welsh marcher lords were active on both sides in the Wars of the Roses (1455 – 85).

During the wars, the Welsh sought a deliverer among the various leaders of the Yorkists and the Lancastrians. The most convincing was Henry Tudor, of an old Anglesey family, the descendant (through his mother's side) of the House of Lancaster. Landing in Wales in 1485, he received considerable support, and Welshmen constituted about a third of his army.

The Welsh fighting spirit had been utilised in the Battle of Bosworth and this won the English crown for Henry VII. By the reign of Henry's son, Henry VIII, most of the marcher lordships had come into the hands of the king, the context of the passage in 1536 of the so-called Act of Union.

The fighting was done; the heroes and anti-heroes are recorded in the annals of history. At various times in life we all take a chance; crossing the road without looking properly or simply standing on a wobbly ladder! You might get knocked over by a passing car or fall off the ladder, but there are no medals if you get hurt!

Transfer this scenario to the realms of sporting heroes and we can see that we could all be up for a winner's medal! To be able to consciously take chances in order to win is the ingredient that sets champions apart from us all. Many of the key figures in history previously mentioned took a chance or two – just think of the treacherous Mordred!

To call Malcolm Price (Pricey) a 'chancer' would be wrong. Pricey has, with premeditated determination, won his battles and hung up his gloves; his story is no less dramatic or tantalising than that of his Welsh ancestors. The energy Pricey channelled into fighting has now been channelled into good. This re-channelling of energy for the betterment of all can be seen to run through Pricey's veins, and was obviously gained from his forebears.

INTRODUCTION

Having covered some of the darker side of Welsh history, it makes it all seem gloom and doom, but what about some of the heroes of the Industrial Revolution? The blood of King Arthur might run through the veins of every Welshman, but equally so does the blood of achievers of greatness.

The Valley of Rhondda might have been plentiful in coal, but 'Merthyr' was the capital of the valleys and supplied something that was to propel the name Merthyr into the new Industrial Age.

In 1750, Merthyr Tydfil was a quiet village surrounded by lush green fields. Most of the 40 or so families who lived in the village worked on the land. However, this situation was to change when it became known that coke could be used for smelting iron. Merthyr Tydfil, with its large supplies of both iron ore and coal, was an attractive site for the ironmasters. Ironmasters from Sussex came into the Welsh valleys and exploited the resources.

As early as 1583, a small works at Pontygwaith was set up and the Dowlais Iron Works was born and went on to become the largest in the world. The local communities supplied men of iron to work the valleys. At first, the ironmasters imported experienced workers from other iron-working areas such as Shropshire. In an effort to persuade these skilled men to move to Merthyr Tydfil, they were offered relatively high wages and good housing.

The ironmasters also needed a supply of unskilled labour from other parts of Wales; they had to build houses for these people. Whereas skilled workers with families were usually provided with four-room terraced houses, unskilled workers were only given one- or two-roomed houses.

Eventually, large numbers of immigrants came into the area from places such as Russia, Ireland and Spain.

Over the course of a hundred years, various names became synonymous with these Iron Works: Thomas Lewis purchased the first lease in 1757 and set up a rather primitive furnace next to Dowlais Brook. Anthony Bacon set up the first furnace at Cyfartha. John Guest successfully managed Dowlais and started supplying some of the cannon used by the British forces in the American War of Independence (1775–1783).

Richard Crawshay leased the Cyfartha Works in 1786, and became sole owner in 1794. When, in 1802, Lord Nelson, the Commander of the British Fleet, paid a surprise visit to the Cyfartha Works in Merthyr Tydfil, Crawshay shed tears of joy and shouted to his workers, 'Here's Nelson, boys; shout, you beggars!'

By 1801, Ynysfach had two blast furnaces built by Thomas Jones of Merthyr Tydfil. These furnaces were large for the period – 53ft in height and had steam-powered blast, which gave a much higher output. Local ore was prepared there. By this time, over 8,000 people were living in Merthyr Tydfil, making it the largest town in Wales.

It is claimed that the first journey by steam locomotive running on rails took place in Merthyr Tydfil in 1804. This journey was made by Richard Trevithick, and was partly brought about as the result of a wager!

By 1830 richer ores were imported to Ynysfach via the

Glamorganshire Canal. After the strike of 1874 the Cyfartha Works were converted to steel production.

In April 1831, riots broke out in Merthyr Tydfil when the House of Lords defeated the proposed parliamentary Reform Bill. The leader of the reform movement in the town was imprisoned but a crowd of 3,000 people surrounded the prison and forced the authorities to release Thomas Llewellyn.

By June, another rebellion followed in which 26 people were arrested and put on trial – two of the men were sentenced to death and several others were transported to Australia. Already, Merthyr was building a reputation as a town not to be messed with and the men were as hard as iron.

By the 1830s, the Dowlais Works was owned by Josiah Guest. The owner of another ironworks near Merthyr Tydfil, Anthony Hill, joined forces with Guest and they formed the Taff Vale Railway Company. A very talented engineer from Bristol, Isambard Brunel, was assigned the job of building the railway.

The Taff Vale Railway was born in 1841. Now it was possible to transport goods from Merthyr Tydfil to Cardiff in less than an hour – Wales was becoming smaller, or so it seemed. Further branches were built, which linked the mining valleys with Welsh ports and England's fast-growing industrial towns and cities. Welsh coal, hewn from the valleys, was profitable enough to be transported to countries as far away as Argentina and India.

As always, there is an anti-hero, and in this case it was the ironmasters who diverted the water from the River

Taff in order to supply their steam engines. As a result the Taff became an open sewer. Outbreaks of typhoid and cholera were common, Merthyr had a poor freshwater supply and by 1848, Merthyr Tydfil's mortality rate was the highest in Wales and the third highest in Britain! Most of the deaths were suffered by children under the age of five. And so the heroes had changed into anti-heroes.

Merthyr Tydfil was the most significant Welsh town of the Industrial Revolution. The industrial landscape (late-eighteenth to nineteenth centuries) is still evident. Merthyr was one of the areas to put up the most resistance to the erection of a Union workhouse – not until 1848 was the Board of Guardians persuaded to undertake this. However, for various reasons, including a cholera epidemic, it was not until the end of 1850 that plans were agreed upon. The firm Aickin and Capes of Islington designed the new building, situated at the east side of Thomas Street in Merthyr. At a cost of £10,000, it was to accommodate 500. Eventually, in September 1853, the workhouse was opened.

Merthyr was supreme in the manufacture of iron until new manufacturing processes demanded much purer iron. Due to this demand, the population decreased, but Merthyr, being full of fight, made a comeback, and the demand for coal helped further expansion. Sadly, the demand for this commodity collapsed in the 1920s.

The last of the great iron works to be built in Merthyr, Penydarren iron works founded in 1784 by Samuel Homfray, closed in 1859. The original Dowlais Works closed in the 1930s, but production continued at the Ifor Works until 1987.

The iron works at Cyfarthfa employed 1,500 people and was said to be the biggest in the world. In 1847, the management's refusal to change to steel production brought about the works eventual closure in April 1874. However, in 1879, the works were converted into a steel production plant and reopened in 1882. By 1910, it again, closed. In 1915 it was reopened to produce pig iron and shell steel during the Great War. Finally, in 1919, it closed forever. The dismantling commenced in 1928.

The Merthyr Electric Traction & Lighting Company operated 16 tramcars, running from Cefn Coed to the Bush Hotel Dowlais, and from Pontmorlais Circus to Graham Street. Opened, Good Friday, 6 April 1901 ... closed, Wednesday, 23 August 1939. By 1945, production levels had dropped by 40 per cent per man since 1880.

Over the decades, there was a huge capital investment to bring about modernisation. Nationalisation offered a new beginning. Coal was becoming the 'dirty' fuel and the coalfield markets collapsed, bringing about the death knell for the coal industry in Wales. Oil and gas put the final nail in the coffin of the coalfields. Coal, once the hero and saviour of the Welsh valleys, had been dropped like a hot potato!

The Aberfan disaster hit Wales like some sleeping Welsh giant awakened in anger at the collapse of the coal industry. At 9.15am on Friday, 21 October 1966 a mining waste tip slid down a mountainside into the mining village of Aberfan, near Merthyr Tydfil, in South Wales.

Children at Pantglas Junior School, situated below the waste tip, had just returned to their classes. Echoes of 'All

Things Bright and Beautiful' had hardly faded away from the morning assembly when the slide started.

First to be destroyed in the path of the slide was a farm cottage, killing all the occupants. The mountain was ablaze with sunshine, but visibility in the village was down to a mere 50 metres.

The rumbling of the giant's stomach could be heard miles away: everything stopped, everyone stopped. Nothing could be seen; soon the Black Death would descend upon the school.

Nothing could be done to stop the slide; a tipping gang on the mountain could do nothing but look on in silent agog. Their telephone line had been destroyed, but even a telephone call would not have saved the loss of 144 lives (116 schoolchildren). The Investigative Tribunal of Inquiry later established that the disaster happened so quickly that a telephone warning would not have saved lives.

Before coming to a rest, the slide had engulfed the school and about 20 houses in the village. Then there was a silence beyond comprehension. Everyone wanted to help, and cars laden with shovels and helpers appeared. Within two hours, all who were to be found alive were pulled free. Nearly one week later, the last of the bodies were recovered. One of the helpers was Malcolm Price.

By 1975, there were only 33,000 coalminers in the South Wales coalfield, and by the 1990s this figure had dropped to the high hundreds. The now-famous picket line strikes of 1973 and 1974, further compounded by the strike of 1984 – 85, put paid to the coal industry. Arthur

Scargill became Lord Scargill. The hero who had stood in picket lines and was once arrested had somehow changed into the well-heeled lord.

This once-proud post-industrial area of South Wales had been cast aside, spurned and left to die. The area had been stripped of its once magical assets that were hewn from deep within its bowels by Welsh pitmen.

To add insult to injury, pit heaps were spewed on to the landscape like giant piles of vomit, strewn inconsiderately near the doorsteps of those who were responsible for digging up the innards of the valleys like graveyards.

A feeling of emptiness must have been left in the pit of this sleeping giant's stomach, as it turned into a forlorn figure. Just like a retired boxer bidding for a return fight and being spurred on by sympathisers to his plight, little chance of a comeback existed.

This sleeping giant was just waiting for any excuse to flex its weary, but not altogether worn-out, muscles, just to show others that it was still capable of putting on a show for the rest of the world to see. The weary giant of the Welsh hills may as well have taken its place next to King Arthur in his resting place, for the Welsh valleys had been raped.

The last great show of Welsh strength was in the 1970s, when Arthur Scargill (Mineworkers' Union leader) was much more accurate with his predictions than those of Nostradamous ever were. Scargill predicted the end of the pits! Scargill's prophecies fell on deaf ears. The pits had been forced to close, with no prospects for employment; the money that had once meagrely filled wage packets had dried up.

The economic damage became clear in 1997 when the number of households in Wales with an income of less than £10,000 per annum had reached 50 per cent. Economic deprivation was to make Merthyr Tydfil the poorest area in Wales with 66.4 per cent of households earning less than £10,000 per annum.

In 1998, on a par with England and Scotland, the weekly average gross earnings in Wales were considerably less at £354. Merthyr Tydfil, the Capital of the Valleys, had become a sad sight. The Iron Capital was once the cradle location of the Industrial Revolution; surely it could suffer no further punishment?

Merthyr Tydfil, no longer the Iron Capital, now prides itself on being the commercial and shopping capital of the Heads of the Valleys region. The economic changes – within such a tight-knit community has taken its toll. The loss of heavy industries has long ceased to play a part in the economic life of Merthyr Tydfil. All that is left is an abundance of heavily subsidised heritage sites, which reflect the town's important industrial past.

Historians may baulk at the interesting historical vistas; tourist offices may admirably point out the doorsteps of some of the loveliest scenery in Wales and the National Park may shout about its Brecon Beacons, but the very people whose veins it runs through are the only ones capable of bringing such a heroic past to life. Tourists cannot ever taste what a Welshman can taste.

The film *Twin Town*, based on the drug culture in Wales, shattered the idea that Wales was a small part of the world solely defined by its history and its dramatic and beautiful countryside. Illegal drugs and murder vaulted the city life of Swansea to the public eye. Gone was the stereotypical but captivating image of 'There'll be singing in the Valleys'. A new challenge to the legendary status of calmness amongst those living in a land once plagued by attacks from all sides of the Welsh borders was to be the start of an insight into what really goes on in Wales.

Enshrined within Malcolm Price is such a Welshman; a man of past and present; a man with a following that could have seen him become a living King Arthur. Just as many of the aforementioned have been perceived as heroes and anti-heroes, Pricey has endured the same label.

Pricey defeats the theory that barbarianism and finesse cannot be rolled into one. The barbarianism was born from his fight to make it in life; his finesse was brought about by his sensitivity to what he was deprived of when he was a child.

Go to Merthyr Tydfil and go cycling, have a picnic, play golf, discover a nature trail, go fishing, visit the large leisure complex, go rambling, take a guided walk, go pony-trekking, play indoor bowls, go sailing, explore Merthyr's rich industrial history, go windsurfing or take a ride on a mountain railway. *But*! Until you have met Pricey, you have never taken in a breath of what Wales and its people are all about.

Born in Merthyr Tydfil, South Wales, Malcolm Price is now in his 50s. As he sits in the living room of his home on one of the toughest housing estates in Europe, the Gurnos Estate, he matter-of-factly reflects on his tough upbringing.

As a child, his father was very strict and made him go to the boxing gym. At first, Pricey didn't want to go ... his father, though, forced him to attend a couple of times a week. Eventually, the training paid off and he won the Welsh Schoolboy Championship.

Pricey went on to turn pro, having had six fights, winning four and losing two. The losing bouts were to the same man, 'Big' Jim Monahan. He was a 'big bugger', about 6ft 4in.

One day, Pricey asked his father if he would pick up his coat, which Pricey had left in the Swan pub the night before. When his father got there, the place was a mess! Pricey had been fighting in there the night before ... his father wasn't too happy. Pricey moved in with his gran.

The bar fight led to Pricey serving six months in prison and he was also stripped of his boxing licence. Freedom was to see Pricey take up part-time bouncing on the pub and club doors, which he enjoyed, although this was not his main occupation.

Growing up in Merthyr, people couldn't help but hear the name 'Malcolm Price'. Everybody had his or her own stories of him. He was and still is a very well-respected man. Although based in Wales, Pricey is well known to those unfortunate enough to have bumped into him when he was working in England and on the Scottish borders.

Stories about this man's physical prowess are in great abundance and, up to now, Pricey has refused to co-operate with the many tempting offers put his way by those wishing to tell his story. TV documentary makers have also been disappointed to find a negative response to their pleas for his help.

INTRODUCTION

Since reaching maturity, Pricey has settled down and prefers a sedentary lifestyle, but stories of his fights just keep going on and on and have made him a living legend and a well-respected figure.

In order to grasp the in-depth picture of this man it would be better to relate some of the more violent events, as told in chapter one, in Pricey's own voice.

Stephen Richards

CHAPTER 1

YOUNG BLOOD

Gradually, the physical cruelty and punishment beatings started and it got worse. He'd be on his knees trying to teach me how to fight, so my father made out. Whack! His hand would slap into my face with the full-force might of a 6ft 4in, 18-stone man!

My mother used to say to him, 'Your hands are too heavy for him, he's only a kid!'

He would bawl back at her, 'Mind your own fucking business, woman, I'm learning him to look after himself.'

My boxing career started when my father forced me to go to the gym. 'You get to that bloody gym,' he would bark at me, 'and you'll learn how to use yourself.' I didn't want to go along. I remember the first time he put me in the ring; he put me under the guidance of Bill Evans. Bill used to take all the kids; he had his own gym down in Merthyr Labour Club.

I remember John Gamble from when a few other kids and me went to the gym. We used to play together down at my gran's house. From there, we used to go to the gym together: two pairs of boots, two pairs of bumpers and some kind of shorts and we were ready.

The first time we were in the gym, that first night, it was all strange. You could smell the smoke and the sweat and the normal odours of the gym, but it was weird to us. He wanted to put me in the ring with Don James. He's now secretary of the Welsh Ex-Professional Boxers Association. He put me in the ring with him, but we were only kids – 11 or maybe 12 years of age.

Anyway, he put me in the ring with Don James, who was older than me, and Don proceeded to knock several kinds of shit out of me. Don was hard and he turned out to be a good boxer – he beat Walter McGowan from Scotland who later went on to become World Champion.

So there I was – my father paying for my boxing lessons – but all I wanted to do was what any normal kid of that age wanted to do. I wasn't allowed to play out and do normal things like that. I used to feel terrible.

At the thought of going to the gym, my insides would quack, my mouth would dry up, I just didn't want to go to these gyms; I was more interested in ornithology – birds. That was the kind of thing I was into from six years of age onwards, and I'm still into birds and wildlife now.

As my boxing progressed, these intense feelings of fear subsided and I started to have a couple of bouts. The first time that I lost and went back home, these feelings of fear that I had when I first started going to the gym had come back with a vengeance! I remember, I walked in to the house expecting to be consoled by my father, but he yelled, 'What, you fucking lost?' At this stage I was still only a kid but if I lost then I was given a good kicking by him. He would suddenly turn into King Kong and proceeded to paint the walls seven colours of shite with me! As a child, I wasn't yet a match for a man's might.

If I lost a bout, I soon learned not to go home straight afterwards – I would give him time to go to the bar first. Even though I'd go to all of that trouble to escape his ranting and raving, my father would come home steaming drunk, drag me out of bed whilst I was still half asleep and beat the living shit out of me! It became too much of a terrifying nightmare for me to bear; it was the nearest thing I can describe to a living hell. My failures were more than just failures; I didn't just get a beating in the boxing ring ... I was literally fighting for my life to avoid a much worse fate that awaited me at home if I lost!

The first year I entered the Welsh Schoolboy Championships, I lost on points in the finals. The second year, I had an almighty row with my father about four or five weeks before the Welsh Championships, and took another hammering and kicking off him. I had a really bad cut underneath my right eye. My mother was up in arms and wanted to get me to hospital – she was all for it, as my eye was badly cut and needed stitching up. My father made it clear that I wasn't allowed to go: 'He don't want no fucking hospitals!' The physical damage gradually healed up itself.

I had more fights – I'd win a couple and then I'd lose one

again! We'd all be in the car, the late Hughie Thomas, brother of the late Eddie Thomas, took us to these tournaments and when he'd be dropping us off he'd take us straight to the door. If I won then, fine, I would ask to be dropped off at the door. When I lost I asked to be dropped off at the end of the street.

It got to the stage where, if I lost, I just didn't want to go home. My father would come home smashed out of his skull again and he'd rant, 'He's not doing good enough at the gym!' You couldn't go to bed and go to sleep, you just had to pretend you were asleep. He'd kick open my bedroom door and then the shakes would come over me and exceed the bounds of any pain I'd ever known. It was a bad feeling.

I'd lie there pretending to be asleep, but it was to no avail. The pretence of sleep was no shield against what would follow. As surely as night follows day, the crash of his foot kicking against my door would be followed by the crash of his foot against my head. Violence and brutality became a way of life for me. Again, the kicking would start and my father would hurl my mother about for daring to intervene.

When I was 11 or 12 years of age, I remember my old man worked long distance for British Road Services, and then he finished for them and he started working on the mountain, the open cast. He used to work long hours, 12, 14 hours a day; he used to be on the dozers and the Euclid dump trucks.

I became an object of ridicule; he would scoff and scorn me and holler out, 'He'll never have any brains; he'll never pass a driving test. He certainly won't be able to drive a machine. He hasn't got the bastard brains!' But, later on in my life, I shocked him when I passed my test first time, and I travelled all over the country and learned to drive most machinery – even earthmoving machines. I did this for myself; I wasn't trying to prove that I was better than him or trying to get his approval. I never enjoyed my father's approval or admiration for all that I achieved ... nothing I did ever seemed to encourage him to drop his unceasing tirade of verbal and physical abuse against me anyway.

When I eventually left Queens Road school, the headmaster was all for me following my hobby of ornithology. He said that I should get a job working with birds. I had a job to go to straight away, as they had gone out of their way to find this job for me and I could have gone to 'Slimbridge', Peter Scott's Wildfowl Trust. (Later, in 1989, it was to become the Wildfowl & Wetlands Trust (WWT).) But I had a job waiting for me so my father wouldn't let me go. He said, 'There's no money in that, birds!'

How I would have loved to be in the employ of Peter Scott and to have learned from him rather than doing what I was forced to do. After founding the WWT, Peter went on to become Honorary Director until his death in 1989, two weeks short of his 80th birthday. To be recognised the world over for such work is far more worthy than to be recognised for standing fighting in the streets as I did.

In 1979, Peter received a knighthood for his work in conservation, but it all started with the World Wildlife

Fund (WWF), which he founded in 1961. The contrast was, Peter was doing the things I would have enjoyed doing, whilst I was forced to take up something else.

This man, Peter Scott, was an amazingly sensitive and caring man. And I know a lot of people are going to say that I'm saying that in such a way because of my father's uncaring and insensitive nature, but that's not true. I didn't look at Peter Scott as a surrogate father figure; I didn't know anything else other than how my father treated me ... period.

I admired the many facets to Sir Peter, but first and foremost he was a naturalist and after that he was a talented painter, broadcaster, global traveller, war hero and Olympic sportsman.

I look back on that missed opportunity to join Sir Peter with enormous sadness, as much as conservation was Sir Peter Scott's passion, so it was and still is mine.

As much as my father was a bastard towards me, Sir Peter's father was an inspiration to him. Scott of the Antarctic, Captain Robert Falcon Scott, was Sir Peter's father. In 1912, when Peter was only three years old, his father left for the Antarctic, only to die there. During the ravages of a blizzard, Captain Scott, dying in his tent, left a letter with instructions about bringing up his son. It read, 'Make the boy interested in natural history if you can. It is better than games.' In contrast to that, my father detested my involvement with nature, his words of support to me were, 'He don't need no fucking hospitals!'

Sir Peter was a true sportsman, at the Berlin Olympics in 1936, which were presided over by Adolf Hitler, he won a bronze medal for single-handedly sailing at Kiel and went on to win the Prince of Wales' Cup for dinghy racing.

Taking after his father, unlike me, he joined the Royal Navy in 1940 as a sub-lieutenant on board HMS *Brooke* and he was mentioned in Dispatches for his part in rescuing the crew of a burning warship in 1941.

In 1942 he was appointed Lieutenant Commander, after receiving an MBE. He followed this up in 1953 when he was awarded a CBE for his role as Honorary Director of the Wildfowl Trust. A great man, indeed.

In between boxing and avoiding my father's boot, I used to smuggle young birds into the house. I had baby owls, and I'd feed them and my mother would say in a fearful way, 'Don't show your father, mind!'

I remember, somebody had given me a raven chick that I reared until he could fly. My mother was fearful that my father would find this raven, which I had hidden in a big cardboard box under my bed! The worries my mother had over my father finding that raven are nobody's business. She told me to let it go in case my father found out.

Eventually, the raven was fully grown and was able to fly, so I let him go. Behind our house, which backed on to a park, there were some big trees. He flew off to the trees and I thought that he was gone for good. They say that if you love something then let it go and if it comes back then it loves you, but if it never comes back then it wasn't to be. In the morning, there he was sitting on the fence calling out for food!

The old man found out that I had him and he whinged on and snapped at me, 'He'll have to go; is he one of yours, a throwaway? If that bird's not gone by tomorrow, I'll borrow a gun and shoot him!' That's how much of a heartless domineering bastard he was! I had an uncle, a war hero, who had won medals in the Second World War, who worked for a forestry company. I took the raven there for safekeeping. I was happy in the knowledge that this raven I had reared from being a half-dead chick to a full-flight thing of beauty would not be shot by my father.

In my bedroom, I had it all; I even had a stuffed fox with a pheasant in his mouth on show in a glass case! I had jays, the raven, a rook and I had a lot of boxes full of birds' eggs that I had collected over the years, many of them given to me by my forestry-working uncle. I was right into ornithology. My mother always said to my father, 'Well, it's his interest, you never know where it will take him.'

Sport played a big role in my schoolboy life, but I seemed to care more about what my friends could have achieved compared to what I was supposed to. My mate John Dee played football for the school, but he didn't follow it up. Why he didn't take it up professionally I'll never know, because his father was a professional football player and he travelled the world, and he was a good footballer. I suppose bearing the same name as the astrologer to Queen Elizabeth I was enough for John Dee.

I seemed to want other people to achieve things; maybe this was my way of copping out. I remember my first boxing match as a schoolboy … I lost. I was young then and I managed to bounce back and win the next time around, and the next one after that too. I suppose the fear of a punishment beating by my father spurred me on to win.

When I became Schoolboy Champion of the whole of Wales, for me it might as well have been the world championship title I had won because that would have done me. I thought that would have been sufficient to quell my father's desire for me to go further in the boxing career that he forced me into, but no.

My father thought it was the world championship, too, the way he went on. Oh aye, he thought the world of that, but not of me! I was a child slave to his own desires. I still don't know why.

I got three feathers for the Welsh Championship. I felt that I had given my father what he wanted and I could now go back to my ornithology, but no! For some fathers, that would be it, wouldn't it? They would be over the moon just to have a son like me. Not my father, though. He then wanted me to go for the fucking next title. 'Stick at it, stick at it,' he would bark at me. He wanted to conquer the world through me by proxy.

I then went on to win the Welsh Youth Championship, then after that I went on to win the Welsh NCB (National Coal Board) Championship. It was all a progression, wasn't it? Leading to the next thing in life.

Eventually, I left Billy Evans's boxing guidance. Gamble and me changed over to Eddie Thomas's club. Eddie Thomas was world famous. As a fighter, he was the Welterweight Champion of Britain, the Empire and Europe, and was briefly the leading contender for Sugar Ray Robinson's world title.

So we moved camp under Eddie Thomas's guidance. Eddie's brothers, who were also boxers, also looked after me. They were a hard, tough and well-respected family.

Hughie used to be up the gym most of the time. I really liked him – he was a hell of a nice down-to-earth fellow, and so was Eddie. He was something a bit special; he was a great and understanding man.

Eventually, I was picked to represent Wales as a senior; I was now a Welsh International! I had to go in for the British ABA Championships; there were certain different ways you could go about getting to the Albert Hall for the British ABA. Our way in was to join the Air Cadets, and there was Gerald Jones and me – he's got his own gym now has Gerald, a fucking good fighter.

We were all under Eddie Thomas together and, at one time, he had all the Welsh champions under his guidance. Everyone had his weight with the Welsh Championship, and he said, 'I got them right all, right down from a heavyweight to the smallest weight.' Under Eddie Thomas a lot of them turned pro.

We joined the Air Cadets, and then Jonesy and me won the Welsh ATC Championship and the British ATC Championship. All the British champions then came together and they called it the British ISBA Championships. There were all the British champions of the Army, the Cadets, the Air Force and the Navy.

We met together at the British Championships in Portsmouth on board HMS *Victory*. That's where I met McGowan. Walter McGowan was this little Scots boy who later went on to become World Champion. I think Jonesy won it, but I'm not sure, but I won my title and that's all that mattered at the time; by winning I could avoid another punishment beating from my father.

I fought a fellow once, they called him the KO Kid; John Joyce was there too. Anyway, we won the British ISBA Championship in Portsmouth. That was a big thing, all up-and-coming stars. We then went on to reach the finals in the Albert Hall, the British ABA. I fought a fellow called John Jennings from West Ham. I was shocked because I thought I had won this contest, you know, but obviously I lost by a razor's edge decision. I thought I'd won it and so did Eddie, but it went the other way and that was it. Of course, it had to be a local London boy who won the title.

After that, I fought for Wales against Luxembourg and Holland. At this stage in my boxing career, I was still a young pup and needed to gain experience to get over my two international losses. I fought against far more experienced and older boxers, but Eddie Thomas wasn't worried about that and he said it was all experience. So it was a stepping-stone for me.

Although I was now representing my country and winning, it wasn't ever enough for my father. Even at this stage of my career, I would come home after losing and he would still go up like a rocket! I thought, Fucking hell! I'm off, and legged it. There was another colossal row in the house as I made my escape through the bedroom window. I was away!

I scrambled out of the window; I didn't want to go to my gran's because she was a good age. She was 94 when she died, and my grandfather was an age as well. My aunty took me in for a while and then I was away. She took me in for a few days until it had cooled down and then I went through the usual routine of going back home. But the thing was, I wasn't going to put up with it any more, so off I went, out the fucking window! I was about sixteen or seventeen years old. I couldn't stick it any more. My mother was up my gran's as well; she too had left him ... albeit temporarily.

I went down to where the corporation buses were parked up and slept in the old colliery bus for about ten days. By this time, my family, except my father, were getting anxious as to my whereabouts. No one had seen me but then, eventually, they found me.

While I was away, my father, in a fit of rage, smashed up all of my birds' eggs, ripped up all of my clothes and tore my Welsh blazer with the three feathers on it to shreds. That was the blazer I'd won for the Welsh Championships, and it was my pride and joy!

The three feathers was a crest of three ostrich plumes and the motto *Ich Dien* (meaning I Serve) and was adopted by Edward the Black Prince at the Battle of Crecy, which took place on 26 August 1346 (The Hundred Years War). The feathers represented the spiritual and temporal power of the ancient Celtic kings and priests. Since that time, in the form of three ostrich feathers, the three golden rays have been borne by successive Princes of Wales.

But, to me, the blazer represented all of the pain and suffering I had overcome at home and I wore it to represent my rites of passage from being a boy to becoming a man. Even though my father wanted me to be a success at boxing, he was a fanatic and a fucking first-class nutcase and a heavy drinker!

I don't know what he wanted out of me ... he wanted

fucking super-boy. If I'd been a bastard of a boy then I would have expected what he dished out to me. I wasn't a burglar, I wasn't a car thief and I wasn't a thief … period! So what was I doing wrong?

My mother eventually returned home to him. I said to her, 'Don't worry, I'll grow up and it won't always be like this.' I wouldn't go through that again for anything, fuck that!

But the things you're supposed to be able to depend on weren't always there for me. It's like when I was going to church. Churches are supposed to be sanctuaries; you could run into a church and the law couldn't come in after you, you were safe. But, today, the doors are never open on a church because it's not safe to leave them open. Before, people could go in and say a quick prayer. But, today, the doors are not left open because of these bastards; they've no respect, they would steal the Holy Cross and think nothing of it.

As I've already said, I didn't know what my father expected of me. I was law abiding as a child and law abiding as an adult in the respect that I wouldn't steal anything. I recall an incident that will show you what I mean. I can't mention any names – we were skint, out of work and it was wintertime.

Once, this fellow came up to me and he said, 'Hey, we've got a big eagle.'

I replied, 'Oh, aye, eagle?' I thought he was on about some kind of an emblem weighing a few ounces.

In a whisper, he said, 'We're gonna melt it down.'

I suddenly twigged as he indicated with his hands to

show the vast size of it as he said, 'His wings are out here as well, like.'

His eyes bulged as he said, 'We can hardly melt it down!'

I replied excitedly, 'We'd have the money then? Aye, all right, I'll go.'

He said, 'Come up to the house and see my friend.'

So off I went up to the house and, when he took this big cloth off the bed to reveal what was underneath it, I said, 'Fucking hell! That's the lectern from the front of the church; they read the testament from that. I want nothing at all to do with it. You'd have no luck with that! You'd better take that back and leave it outside the church – that's thieving, that is. You can't take it nowhere.'

Anyway, they took it back and planted it, left it outside the undertaker's home, and they had to give it back to the church.

So that was that, and one of the lads that took it never had a day's luck in his fucking life after that. Funny that, isn't it?

I've never been a thief, not to this day. I might have taken a bit of diesel oil for one of the lads that was a bit short, or whatever, but I am not a thief. If I found a pound on the floor in a pub I would put it on the bar and say, 'Someone has lost a pound here.' And that is the way it was and that is the way I've gone through life. I've never been a thief in my life and that is the truth.

I was about 30 years old when the eagle incident happened, but my childhood choirboy days gave me reverence and respect for the church. The incident with the eagle must have been when I was at home in between motorway jobs. They used to pay you off from earthmoving jobs in the winter, once the bad weather was back, and then give you a call or whatever when it became dry.

I was with Colin Garcier and Mike Mahoney once when Mahoney stopped for a fag; he was leaning against this shop door because it was raining and the door just flew open! The shop was closed, no one was in the place and it was full of these toys. Colin Garcier walked in and he said, 'Look at these things here!' Dump trucks and things! I wanted nothing out of the place and I said, 'That's thieving.' We all walked off and left the place as we found it.

I was always mature enough to know that stealing gets you nowhere. I always have been. I would walk into a church and the hairs on the back of my neck would stand up; I don't know why. Possibly because it's a gothic-looking place. My father had no reason to complain about police coming to the door about me, I was a model child and someone he should have been proud of.

My parents weren't really God-fearing church-going people. My mother used to go to church now and again, but nothing like I was doing. I think my gran and grandfather on my mam's side were chapel-going people years and years ago.

Although my father had trouble coming to terms with the ornithology side of things, he had no qualms about me being in the church choir – he didn't mind that at all. I used to go to church, Saint David's, in Merthyr. My photo still hangs there in the vestry. I did well under the guidance of the choirmaster and organist W J Watkin. He's got big letters after his name: he was well up the ladder in society.

He was a personal friend of Sir Malcolm Sergeant. Yes, he was right into music, used to teach everyone in Merthyr and the outer areas – they all used to go to him.

Welsh mezzo-soprano, Olwen Price (1903–1999), who came from Merthyr Tydfil, began to study singing privately at the age of 18 with W J Watkins. Olwen could sing anything from Mozart to Menotti, Verdi to Vaughan Williams. Much of her career was spent with Sadler's Wells' Opera and she also sang for the BBC, once assisting the great tenor Beniamino Gigli in a recital, and with the Welsh National Opera. The Blue Ribbon awarded to the best solo vocalist at the National Eisteddfod of Wales, held that year at Machynlleth, and also the prize for the contralto solo went to Olwen Price.

My father made me go in the choir, and I would be there morning and evening. I had to go to Sunday school as well. I had to go three times every Sunday. I kind of liked singing and I used to like the sound of the huge organ. We sang from Mendelssohn as well as 'Handel's Messiah'. Unbelievable, isn't it? It was good that I had a good voice as well. Little Gwyn Owen and me, we sang 'O, for the wings of a dove', Mendelssohn. I also sang some anthems from the Messiah as well.

Even though we were choirboys, we still used to get up to some mad tricks and the usual schoolboy pranks; we used to stick chewing gum on each other and on each other's salters. We had lots of fun; we used to go on trips to the seaside at Mumbles and Porthcawl, all the choirboys together and all the tenors and baritones and all that. We used to have great times and, if we didn't have a ball, one of the boys would pick one up from somewhere and we would go on the beach and play cricket. They were good times.

My musical taste seems to have stemmed from being a choirboy. Operatic tenors and choral singing are my favourites, probably, some would say, this was typical of someone with a Welsh heritage. We used to go to Hereford Cathedral every Sunday. I like to hear the organ and I like to hear the choir singing. I have a lot of time for the operatic tenors. My music collection comprises of the Three Tenors – I've even got the King of Tenors, Enrico Caruso. There are some great tenors in the world, one of my favourites being Andrea Bocelli.

I have an affinity with Caruso, who was born on 27 February 1873 in Naples, Italy. He, like me, was born into a working-class family and into a working-class neighbourhood. Caruso was born to a family of singers; I was born to a man of violence! My father was a manual worker, as was Caruso's, and both our fathers were heavy drinkers. Just like I was forced to attend boxing classes, Caruso was forced by his father to attend singing lessons.

And, just as I had an interest in something other than what I was forced to do, Caruso had an interest in drawing. But there was one big difference between Caruso and me: Caruso had the courage to deceive his father about attending school when he bunked off to go and play with his friends. But Caruso's father had a mean streak, just like my father! When he found out about Caruso bunking off school, he forced Caruso to give up his education to work full-time at a factory.

Other similarities between Caruso and me are uncanny, but that's another story. Although, when you consider that Caruso was the first recording artist in history to clock up a million-seller record, it makes you wonder where some of the crap played on radios today comes from.

Caruso's portfolio included about 60 operas, mostly in Italian, although he also sang in French and English. He could perform some 500 songs, ranging from classical to traditional Italian folk songs to popular songs of the day.

I reminisce about the time I wanted to become a tenor. I was right bang into it but, when my voice broke, my soul broke and I didn't want to go up into the choir. Eventually, I wouldn't have been able to go anyway.

I was ten years old, and us boys didn't know this, but we were voice trained for nothing; you get the voice trained for free. They taught us how to pronounce words, and I really enjoyed it. It was disciplined equally as well as boxing was, but this singing was more of a love for me than the chore of being in the boxing ring.

Boxing and singing in a choir, it's the same and a different thing. You've got respect for the church and then you have the respect for fighters that are at the gym. How could you compare Enrico Caruso to Mohamed Ali? You've got a hard choice there. By all accounts, you might choose Ali; he was the best of all time they reckon ... but so was Caruso!

My relationship with my mother was marvellous. I had a remarkably understanding and loving mother. She was a very kind and giving person and used to help my grandfather out by serving in his fruit shop. I recall my mother working in the shop. Even when she had pleurisy she was a hard-working woman; she worked straight through it. She was a very benevolent person too. If a tramp was passing by, she'd shout out, 'Old man of the road!' She would do up a package, full of fruit, and run after him with it. Doesn't happen now.

As much as my mother was a wonderful lady, my father was the total opposite. I was the school goalkeeper for Queens Road, but the old man kept on at me about the gym and I had to stick with the gym. Although he didn't go to the gym, he wanted me to learn to use myself, to use my hands. He wasn't looking out for my future so as I could use it for my defence, he wasn't a man like that, no! He was just a strict disciplinarian: 'If I say, You go to the gym, you go to the fucking gym and that's that,' he would bawl at me.

I instinctively knew that my father didn't have my interests at heart; how I knew that ... I just don't know. In later years, I believed he wanted me to do the boxing just so as he could tell people about me. He wasn't telling people the usual things that a proud father would normally say of his son; it was more along the lines of what I could do to anyone who stepped out of line! The old man didn't give a fuck, he wanted me to do the hard things all the time; to harden me up. But I was a quiet boy, and I was a shy boy. I didn't need any of this forced on to me, but what could I do – I was trapped!

Some people hear the story about Sir Richard Branson's mother chucking him out of the car when he was six years old. She told him to find his own way back home! Fucking hell, people go on about how cruel that was, but she was doing the boy a favour by building up his self-resourcefulness, if only I had a father who was as kind to me as she was to her son then maybe I would be a billionaire like he became.

Ever since I can remember, even before I went to my first school, Pontmorlais County Junior, I was an introverted and shy child. On my first day at school, I was pretty nervous and jumpy. I remember reluctantly letting go of my mother's hand. That warm feeling of comfort and safety slipping away as our fingers parted!

That warm, safe feeling that my mother gave me seemed to be lost in my dizzy abandonment at what unknown perils I faced as I trudged through the school gates. It wasn't long before I broke the ice with everyone and had my first schoolyard fight; after that I got on pretty well with everyone at school.

Back then, you had a lot of respect for all the teachers. You looked up to them, but it wasn't out of fear, it was out of respect, pure respect. Today, though, it's not like that at all. Ahh ... they cheek the teachers, there is no caning now, is there? Nothing like that is allowed. But the pupils are allowed to do all and sundry to the teachers without any recourse against them. If the parents give their permission for caning to be carried out against their child then it should be allowed, but political correctness doesn't allow for that.

I believe the way of the cane did them a bit of good, yeah, did us a bit of good. Such a thing today would be classed as brutality, but we lived with it and accepted it as normality ... it's only when things like caning become outlawed that it manifests itself into a cruel and violent memory. I was caned many a time.

Christ, I cannot remember the amount of things I was caned for. I do recall the actual caning, though; and it wasn't very a pleasant affair! We got it on the hands. After that, though, you got used to it. The ring stings soon became an accepted part of being taught right from wrong. Look around us in society today – the cane is banned and assaults by pupils against teachers have risen – a connection or what! The prison population is bursting at the seams: how has it come about? The correlation between the banning of corporal punishment and rising crime is clear to see.

I'm not advocating corporal punishment, but the threat of it can be a deterrent. Mind you, ask me to carry out such a punishment on a child and I just couldn't do it! My unhappy memories of a much more sinister type of physical abuse inflicted on me by my father would come flooding back, I'm sure of that.

I was always well behaved for the school music lessons and the gym. On the yard, we used to play football; now I hear that the schoolyard is a place used as a meeting place for kids selling drugs. Kids selling other kids drugs! Kids grow up with a wealth of the wrong type of knowledge, but what's done to shield our children from it?

My time at school helped me overcome problems at home. As we grew up, many of my schoolyard friends went to live away. Good friends like Georgie Jaygo. I had a few fights with George; he's up in London somewhere now. I had quite a few fights after lessons were over and when we were on the way home, all minor skirmishes.

Daft as it may sound, I wasn't into fighting; it just seemed to happen! And then, after the fights, we'd still be mates. It was a normal kind of childhood. Looking back to that time, it seemed that trouble always found an easy route to my door. One of the hurdles faced by some of my peers never seemed to find its way to me – bullying! As for being bullied at school, no, I can't say I was. My only experience of school bullies was in the next school up.

I wasn't very good at the academic subjects at school; I didn't like forcing my mind to do something that it couldn't accept or get into. I believe that we are born with genes that dictate how good we'll be at whatever it is we do and, if we listen to ourselves, we'll find out what it is we're good at.

Just as being a bully must be stamped in certain people's genes, I also believe that being a good boxer or opera singer is also stamped into a gene. We used to play football in the yard, but the older boys used to bully the younger boys; not a great deal of bossing, but they used to tell us to piss off and fuck off and all that, you know? It's normally common in every school, isn't it?

The older boys in the school knew a little about being bullied from being new starters at that particular school themselves; it just happens naturally. I was not a believer in being a bully; I was not that kind of boy. My genes were saved from being stamped with my father's bullying chromosomes. Some of the other boys used to be involved in bullying, yeah. Of course, we'd all been through it – that was accepted.

Schools now, with the philosophy they have on anti-bullying and so on, are maybe going over the top. I don't really know what's changed in schools now, but I believe that they should keep them in order and should have the cane available as a deterrent. Why not? It shows them a bit of respect. The pupils should have respect for the teachers. I believe that some sort of discipline within society has been lost, yes, I do. It's like a different era altogether now, isn't it?

There's no respect for older people at all today, and that's saddening. Look at the way crime against older people has risen! You know, there's no calling people 'Mr' or 'Mrs' now; they just call you, and it's all 'fuck off' and the like.

The drug culture, it's out there. If they could have fished out the drug dealers at an early age before they even became drug dealers and they had someone like my old man, they wouldn't have ended up like that. He would have put them in line and I mean in line! My old man, Les Price, was a very strict man, indeed, he was an out and out disciplinarian and he was way over the top. I wasn't comfortable with his discipline. He was definitely overly strict; he ruled with an iron rod!

When he said 'no', he meant 'no' and there was no answering him back! There was a stage when there was some rebellion from me. I remember back to when I was 14 or 15 years old, I had to be in the house by nine o'clock at night. My upbringing was very tough and I wasn't very happy about it. There were no good times with him; he was a heartless and cold man. For me, that level of assertive firmness wasn't normal. A lot of my friends were allowed out until about eleven o'clock at night, but not me!

The thing is, no child should be afraid to return home if he's lost a boxing contest! I hear that they are on about banning School Sports Day because it's cruel to those who lose or those kids who are useless at sport! Come on, this is ridiculous. What about the kids who are forced to do exams and fail, isn't that humiliating because they can't keep up with their peers? Isn't it degrading to see the results posted up on a school notice board for all to see? Humiliating! Degrading! And they want to ban School Sports Day?

As a young fellow I wouldn't have cared about the humiliation of losing, I'd be more afraid of going home because, apart from the beatings, I wasn't allowed out of the house as a punishment for losing. My father would roar, 'You're supposed to be training hard!' I didn't mind because it was sport, but, the thing is, I didn't want all this shit that came with it. I wanted to be out seeing the birds in the sky and walking in the fields. I was just a schoolboy. I just loved nature, and they could do fuck all with me at school.

I wasn't rebelling against not being able to stay out until eleven o'clock; I was rebelling against the brutality of discipline and restraint. Some people would say it was a normal son and father thing, but the rows that took place in the house are nobody's business. The old lady would always stick up for me.

My mum, Gladys Price, was a lovely understanding lady and, often, she'd have to intervene between my father and me. She would scream, 'Leave it go,' and I'd sit down. My aunty Kyra, my father's sister, who's not long died, was a good person as well and very kind, as was my uncle Joe. They took me in a few times when I was having rows in the house.

My father used to look at my hands to see if there were any signs of nicotine stains on them, and he'd say through his gritted teeth, 'Don't you start fucking smoking!' The first time I ever started smoking was the first time I was in prison. I had a bastard of a toothache when I was banged up in my cell and one of the boys said, 'You should smoke with that. It acts like aspirin water.'

My aspirations never lay with boxing, but that's the way I was pushed. I was still a choirboy when I started boxing because I remember I went to choir practice every Wednesday night. I missed some Wednesday nights if I was boxing and then, when I missed it, I'd have to tell the choirmaster why. I had a battle between the choir and boxing. When my voice inevitably broke, boxing won.

CHAPTER 2

WILD ONE

I wanted to go in one direction but my father forced me to follow his direction, and, somehow, he won. In one of these compelling situations, he wanted me to join the police force, but he had previously said that I didn't have the bastard brains to pass my driving test. What a contradiction in terms.

Years later, to prove my father wrong, I remember the first time I ever set foot in a giant earthmoving machine, a motor scraper. I'd never seen a motor scraper before in my life, but I learned to drive and operate it. One of the fellows on site, a banksman, was in front of me, guiding me with hand signals. He was indicating with his fingers that the digging depth should be two inches, and I can do all that sort of formation now. When you can drive any machine to formation, then you're a driver, and you're special when you can take it to formation.

Knowing how far to drop the blade becomes second nature; you and the machine become one, like nature. You're changing the environment, working for the betterment of others and gaining a sense of achievement. That was something my father couldn't give or instil in me.

I remember one afternoon my father ordered me to: 'Write a letter, now! An application to join the police force.' I must have been about 17 or 18 years old, and I couldn't write that damn letter. I couldn't spell very well.

Eventually, I managed to write the letter of application to join the police force. My mother knew I was missing food over the worry I was going through, but I gained solace by going out looking for birds' nests for eggs and just looking at and watching birds. I was at my happiest when I was doing that. I was out of my father's reach and I could be myself. Often, I'd be in a state of abandonment when I was in this situation; time just didn't seem to matter. And then I'd be brought back to reality as I returned to the world that my father dominated.

My father was always suppressing the softer side of my nature and it seemed to have disappeared in the course of those boxing lessons. My father took away the real me and replaced all that I could have been by imposing his brutal regime of terror upon me.

I wasn't one to throw my weight around, nor do I today, and I don't even like swearing in front of women, so if any women are reading this then I apologise for some of the language I use – it's just man's talk.

Perhaps what happened in an incident after my father forced me to write that letter of application to join the police force was down to my resentment of him, but it certainly ended any chance I had of joining the police force.

One night, I was in Merthyr town and, I had just bought a bag of three pennyworth of chips. Back then, I used to take the groceries out to my grandfather on a Friday after school, after he'd finished work in the fruit shop. I would take the fruit shop orders out to different houses on a trolley on a Saturday morning and then I'd get my pocket money.

Anyway, as I was standing there eating my chips, this policeman comes strolling up to me. I'd never been in trouble in my life before this night. I was stood at this doorway waiting for it to quieten down in the town, waiting for the bus, and I kept my head down. I couldn't understand why he picked on me or why he didn't tell the noisy crowd further down the road to fuck off.

Then, out of the blue, he said to me, 'Right, move on.'

I said, 'I haven't done no harm.'

The policeman scowled, 'You know, when I say "move", you'll fucking move!'

I don't know what came over me, but I chucked the chips at him and I gave him three pennyworth of my boot in his bollocks! There were police all over the place. Mind you, the copper I kicked in the balls wasn't able to blow his whistle for a while! The police, well, they came from everywhere. I had just had enough of everyone. That was the first charge I ever faced, assaulting the police.

Enough was enough, and in the back of my mind I knew I wasn't going to be pushed around any more. Whether I did this as an act of rebellion so as to hurt my father, I don't really know, but I guess it lay in that direction.

This was my first of many trips to the police cells. I remember, in the middle of the night, they must have phoned my father, because some of the police – in fact, lots of the police – knew my old man. So they got in touch with the old man. I don't think we had a phone then so they must have gone to the house and said that they had me locked up, so down he waltzes to the police station.

I could hear his voice raised in anger from where I was down below in the prehistoric dungeon-type cells of the old police station. 'Fucking hell, assaulting the police,' he said and he took me out by the ear and dragged me back home.

After that, I left again and my gran took me in. I thought, Fuck this, I'm definitely not fucking staying and that's it. So I lived with my gran and my aunt Mary. At that time my aunt wasn't married, so she was able to take care of my ageing grandfather, my mother's father, because he was bedridden.

Even though my grandfather was bedridden, he liked singing and was a comical man. He was a real Welsh man and used to talk in Welsh and he used to sing the 'Alleluia' chorus. He had been in the choir years and years ago before I came along. He'd be singing to his heart's content and then my gran would go into the room downstairs and sit at the back of the sitting room and she'd plead, 'Stop this bloody row.'

He used to say, 'Get back to the kitchen, woman, where you belong.' They were happy times for me.

The turning point in my life happened when I was living with my grandparents. I was in my grandfather's fruit shop when the old man came in! He got hold of me in a vice-like grip and he started to pull me out. 'You're coming home,' he growled through gritted teeth. He was pulling at me, trying to tear me out of the shop.

That was it. I let fly with a pounding hook from my left fist and it landed on his jaw. Down he went like a sack of spuds!

The tables had turned. Now it was my turn to be King Kong and he was Mickey Mouse! He went to get back up, but my grandfather stood between us and, in any case, my old man was shaken by what I had just done.

'I'll sort you out,' he mumbled whilst holding his jaw.

My grandfather cut in, 'Oh, yeah, how?'

'I'll get the police on to you,' my old man moaned.

I stood there laughing and he turned and skulked out of the shop.

Even at my wedding, he never turned up but my mother was there, which was important.

Years later, I used to go the Ex-Serviceman's Club and by then he'd somehow mellowed; he knew I was too big and strong for him to handle the way he used to. I wouldn't usually go near his house but, sometimes, if he was ill, I used to call in and see if he was all right, but that was it. My sister, though, looked after him and she never had a finger laid on her by him; she was the apple of his eye.

Eventually, my old man had to go into hospital; my sister and brother-in-law didn't have a car and their son, who was a supply teacher and did have a car, was away, so I had to take her down to hospital to see him. Reluctantly, I went into the hospital with my sister a few times. But once he started swearing I would walk out.

We were at the hospital on the Monday or Tuesday and

we could hear him coughing, he had a loud old bark of a cough. The curtains around his bed were drawn, and the nurse asked us to wait in the office, as the doctors were with him and they would only be about five or ten minutes at the most. Ten minutes later, a doctor walked in and said, 'Sorry, we've lost him!' My sister was stunned; he'd died on the spot while we were there.

I remember at the funeral, I thought, 'What the fucking hell am I doing here?' The brutal shadow of my father had now disappeared from my life.

CHAPTER 3

MALCOLM PRICE GBH

Eventually, I became a pro boxer, first boxing at light heavyweight. My last amateur fight was against Peter 'Rocky' Nelson – I won. This spurred me on to become a pro, and Eddie Thomas was all for it. In my first professional fight, I was billed to fight Steve Walsh, who was from up the country, but I ended up fighting a guy called Carlton Prince Crowler, a big black lad from London, and I think it was his first pro fight, too. I won that; I knocked him clean out. So there I was, winning my first fight as a pro and I was just on the cusp of the pro circuit.

Even though I had just turned pro, I still liked to get out for a drink or two and spend the night gallivanting around, painting the town red. I was in the pub one night, the Swan, and there was a bit of trouble. One fellow called me a 'fucking get' and he went on to push me out of the way, so I gave him a fucking bang straight on the button and down he went like a new road being laid out for all to walk on. He was lying there with his broken teeth shining through his burst lips like the glimmering cats' eyes on a motorway.

I grabbed at my half-empty glass and smashed it off the bar counter, sending a shower of glass and beer all over the place. Without a second thought, when he was down on the ground, I gave him a glass pie in the face, a swiping blow! Even though he tried to move away, I was too quick for him. The crowd and the place went crazy! I didn't know how many were there with him or what would happen next. I was in fighting mode and at my most dangerous!

Afterwards, I knew in my mind that I shouldn't have done that; it was the wrong thing to do and how I kicked myself for doing it. My testosterone levels must have been full to overflowing. I had the man on the ground and should have just put the boot in. After this incident, I just used to give them the taste of leather from my footwear ... well, apart from one other time!

I just thought this man I set about with the glass had a scratch on him, as he only bled a little bit. I didn't stick him directly in the face or anything; it was just a quick reaction, which I thought was one of self-defence. I thought that if he couldn't get up then that was the best way to deal with it; I still don't know why I did that. I was rightfully booked for malicious wounding, but I shouldn't have done that – it fucked me all to pot.

It was heaving in the pub that night and all the glasses were flying about like confetti; everyone started to fight everyone else. The place was a wreck; you could hear the glasses and the bottles flying about.

Malakey Mullins, an old Irish fellow, was keeping it. He was one of the best people I've ever met and, Christ, I didn't think that all the pub was going to start, but it did and every fucker was fighting! There were chairs going over your head and bodies were flying everywhere. That night, they wrecked the place!

The fight started when a man told me to get out of his way when I was stood at the bar; he had an accent and I knew he wasn't from Merthyr.

I said, 'Who the fucking hell are you to shout at me like that?'

Then he went at me with his arm. I said again, 'Who the fucking hell do you think you are?' and that was it, I just banged him and down he went.

After that, I was in demand by pub and club owners and I started doing a lot of bouncing around at a lot of different clubs. I was in real demand. I remember this time I was called on to sort out some trouble in a club in Ponty.

I was told that this big karate guy and his mates were causing trouble there and they were too hard for the local boys to sort out. So, this night, I breezed into the place and I asked the owner to point out this troublemaker and his pals.

There they were, sitting down and drinking. I strolled casually across to the group, picked up a nearby stool and smashed it down on to this big guy's head. I knocked this troublemaker out like a light and his head was well bashed in.

I said to the rest of this fellow's mates, 'Anyone else want the same?' This fellow's mates are shitless and too scared to make a move to help him. I said, 'That will be the end of the trouble then, boys,' and I walked off and never had to be called back to deal with them again.

The malicious wounding charge stemming from the glassing soon caught up with me and I was given six months' imprisonment, which wasn't a bad result. Nowadays such a charge would warrant at least a three- or four-stretch, so I was damn lucky at six months.

I had been in a lot of trouble down the street before that with my street-fighting antics. I can't recall my first street fight, but it would have taken place on a Friday or Saturday night, as that's when things began to happen.

I remember one fellow, I was hitting him and his head crashed straight through a shop window down in Aberfan. Whilst I was working this man over, his wife was jabbing me with the pointed end of her umbrella. The fight happened because when we got up to dance, this well-built guy hit one of my mates who was smaller than him.

The fight I had with him took place out in the street, and his head was put neatly in to the shop window; a television shop – I got booked for the window, the assault and heaven knows what else. The man's face, when I finished with him, looked like crumpled paper! I've had loads of street fights since then, too many for me to remember.

My professional boxing career was now firmly on hold, in fact, I had my boxing licence revoked because of the outstanding malicious wounding charge. Eventually, after a couple of years and a lot of fighting and keeping my nose clean, I got my licence back. I had to buckle down and stop the malarkeying about that I was getting involved in.

But, somehow, I just couldn't keep my nose clean. This time I was down in Porthcawl and went into this pub with about five of my mates from Merthyr. We were staying over for a week of boozing. There was Mike Mahoney, Ginger Harris, Roy Elliott and a few other boys. Sat at the far end of the bar was a pro boxer, a Welsh Champion, who shall remain nameless to save him embarrassment, who was due to fight for the British title. This boxer had a run-in with a fellow who had his girlfriend with him.

The boxer said to the fellow, 'I'm giving you, now, five minutes to fuck off out the pub or I'll knock you all around the pub!' The boy he was talking to was embarrassed, as he knew who was talking to him, and he drank up his pint and fucked off out of the bar. With this, the boxer's mates were laughing.

Five minutes later, I went over to the boxer's table and I said, 'Hey, fuck face! I'm giving you five minutes to drink that pint up and fuck off out or I'm going to kick you all around this fucking bar.'

I returned to the table where my mates were sitting. Mike Mahoney said, 'Pricey, leave it go.' But, after four minutes, the boxer was up, gone, and his mates followed him. All that week, any pub I went into, if the boxer was there, he'd get up and leave.

I just hate bullies and this man was throwing his weight around, so I just gave him a taste of his own medicine. He shouldn't have shamed the fellow the way he did in front of his woman. The fellow wasn't a fighter or anything like that, he was just a normal bloke. Just because this man was a Welsh champion having a shot at the British title didn't mean two monkeys to me, and he knew it. It's one thing to have a fight in the ring, but on the cobbles is a different matter!

. I had just come out of prison and I was ultra-fit and I'd just got my boxing licence back. This boxer was going to end up in hospital for a week or two if he hadn't walked out of the bar and he knew it. Why fight for the British title and then pick on someone who couldn't even put on a boxing glove?

They all knew I was in Porthcawl, as I was renowned in the valleys. We'd heard that there was a new Indian restaurant in town. There weren't that many Indian restaurants around then and this one was new so we thought we'd give it a try. After about a half-hour of being there, somebody started and I knocked him out cold.

I went to go for his pal, but he ran out of the place. I sat back down and finished my grub. When I got up after the meal and went outside, there was this fellow who had run out of the restaurant earlier; he was standing there in the middle of the street with a 12-bore shotgun!

'Look, Pricey, look at this,' said Mike Mahoney.

The fellow standing there with the gun said, 'I know you, you're Malcolm Price. If I kill you, I'll get away with it. You put a hand on me this week in this town and I'll come for you and kill you. I'll fucking shoot you because it's the only chance I've got against you! I could kill you and get away with it!'

I said, 'Fair play, boy. Go on, fuck off.'

I wasn't daft; I knew I couldn't fight buckshot, so I had to leave it go. If I'd felt in the mood then who knows what I would have done, gun or no gun. I admired the boy's pluck, though.

In my second pro fight, I think I fought Billy Wynter, another big muscular black guy: Billy Wynter was put down as Joe Bygraves's double because he looked just like him. I think I stopped him in the fourth or fifth round.

There's only one fellow I lost to, and that was an Irishman, big Jim Monaghan. I had him rocking in one round and after that I had him rocking for another round. He shouldn't have lasted out. I think I caught him on the hop.

Big Jim Monaghan – he used to be a bouncer as well. He was a big hairy bastard; it was like being in the ring with a bear, he even looked like a grizzly bear.

The first fight I had with Jim was at a sporting club in London. It was all posh tables and a dickey-bow job. The fight went the full distance, yeah. The second time I met him, it was up in Manchester; I had him reeling and he was ready to go down. I thought he would go another round and Eddie Thomas said, 'He's ready, he's there for you now.' Fuck me, but I just couldn't fucking catch the bastard. The fight went all the way to the wire and was on points again.

After this, I had more trouble and more street fights and I lost my boxing licence for the second and final time; you don't get it back after the second time. That was the end of my boxing career. Eddie Thomas rightfully called me a 'stupid idiot', but he never lost touch with me. I might as well have put the letters 'GBH' after my name, that's how much trouble I used to get into.

In those days it was either wounding or GBH that I was arrested for, always one of the two. I went to prison down the foundry a few fucking times because I was always fighting. What the hell was I fighting against? Was it the people I injured or the situation I was trapped in?

I know that I wasted myself in those street fights; I could have made a real killing on the pro-fight circuit. I had a total of six pro fights, won four and lost the two I've already mentioned on points to Jim Monaghan.

The Roy Seward fight down in Ebbw Vale was the strangest fight of them all. He was the ex-Midlands Area Champion; I stopped him in the fourth or fifth round. This guy was eventually certified and sectioned off to Broadmoor Asylum where he made a protest on the roof.

I remember he hit me after the bell. He was a strange guy and he was mumbling gibberish all the time he was in the clinches. I kept telling him to 'fuck off'. He was funny, really, but he was a strong guy. Laugh, I laughed all the way back to my corner and we pushed and powered each other – he'd push and I'd power him.

I was gonna kick him up the arse after he threw one at me after the bell. I half turned to give him one, but the ref stepped in between us – even then, I raised my leg to get round the referee to kick Seward up the arse. But Eddie Thomas went fucking crazy, and he shouted in my ear: 'You're not on the road now, you know, you're in a fucking boxing ring! What's the matter with you?'

The crowd went berserk because they didn't like the crack. Anyway, I stopped the lad and that was that.

The wages as a pro boxer back then were very little. You

didn't earn much in your professional career as an up-and-coming fighter. Even the winning fee would only be about £50 or £60. Obviously, if you won the big one then you were made.

Funnily enough, I came to my best when I lost my licence! Then I wanted to fight. I wanted to box. I had more interest than I had so far in my fight to get up the ladder. I was about 22 or 23 years of age when I had my licence taken off me, and I was just starting to get into the swing of things. Losing my licence was daunting. As Eddie Thomas said, 'A boxer doesn't come into his own until he's between 25 and 30 years of age.' Just as I was starting to get ripe and ready I was out of the ring.

I was also holding down a job working on the Heads of the Valley road at the time. So, unlike the boxers of today, I was working 12 hours up there and then going straight to the gym after finishing work. That was unbelievable; boxers now just don't lift a finger, do they? My stepping-stone to glory had turned into a slippery slope of self-destruction. Things have changed dramatically now.

When I found out that I wasn't going to be allowed to box any more, that was it, wasn't it! I felt a bit lost, really. I always kept myself pretty fit, but there was one time when I went up to seventeen-and-a-half stone; I was boozing all the time to numb the pain. I was a heavy drinker and a heavy smoker and then, when you're not boxing, you lose it all.

I had been steered into this career, a career I didn't really want, and yet it became all that I had. Now it had been taken away from me, I had no real reason to steer clear of trouble. I felt betrayed; I was led into something and then let go on my own. I was an accident waiting to happen! My life was a mess.

I must have had that Bugsy Malone type of face that attracts every fucker to have a go at me. And there was the bouncing as well! Although I was in demand for bouncing work after the Swan pub fight, I had actually started bouncing much earlier than this when I was living with my gran at the age of 17. My first bouncing venue was in the Palace Dance Hall, which eventually became a casino.

A man by the name of Mr Hilliard was in charge of the Sands Club; he was a Londoner. We had great times there. He used to say, 'Is everything all right?' and I'd say, 'Sound.' Simple dialogue, but with lots of meaning. There were six of us bouncing for the Sands Club.

I bounced down there and there was this fellow came up to see me. He was having a lot of trouble down in Ystalyfera way and, funnily enough, outside this nightclub he said, 'Wanna come and work for me?'

I said, 'What's the money like?'

He told me the amount; I argued for more. At that time, I had an old Mercedes, a lovely car, but I only had £65 in cash. There were plenty of opportunities to make money and this sort of lucrative offer of being a trouble-shooter was always welcome – they paid for the best and they got the best. When gangs of thugs and liberty-takers were causing trouble, I would be called in to sort things out after everyone else had fled.

I was bouncing at the bottom of town for a while as well. The Bandy Bridge nightclub, I used to bounce there as well. I used to do some work for Elwyn Morgan in between boxing when he ran dances. When I first started bouncing, there were scuffles: you'd find out who the liberty-takers were and put them out cold.

I was in a fight one night; it was a big fight and somebody else started fighting, then somebody else started fighting and they were chucking blows at me. Fuck this, I thought, and punched them. They would punch you back and then people started to go down. From that day on, people started going down and I thought I'm not fucking standing by. Sometimes I tried to talk them out of it as well.

I've got to say, I may have hit people that I shouldn't have hit, people that weren't involved in these fights, but you haven't got time to look around and ask: 'Were you involved with that?' Sometimes you just didn't have time to get the facts, d'you know what I mean? And I apologise if I hit people who weren't involved in the fights. If they put their hands up to me, it was fucking fatal! To anyone who was putting their hands up you would think it was going to be a fight, and I had quick-fire reactions.

I was bouncing down in Bandy Bridge, and I remember this group were at the front of the queue, and they were out for pure trouble: you knew they were out for pure trouble because they were calling us 'Welsh bastards' and heaven knows what else. These men had been coming into Wales out of their territory. They would stand in a nightclub, see the new bouncers and call them 'Welsh bastards'. It was like waving a red rag at a bull! You had to be seriously disturbed people to do that. Yeah, they wanted fucking trouble and that's what they had. It was a bit pricey, though, because one of the guys went smashing through the door.

I shouldn't have gone through the door to the outside, as I was supposed to deal with it inside; but I thought, fuck him, so I went out and put the fucking fear into him. I could hear people shouting, 'He's a fucking animal.'

They only want to come inside and kick some poor fucker to fucking hell in there. Like Lenny McLean said, and I agree with him totally, he told me it's these bastards that hurt the old people and fuck up the young kids; they are the animals and they hardly get any prison sentence for it. There are people in prison now that are laughing at what they have done to people and, fucking hell, the system is all to cock.

What's life like? It's all to hell. They talk to a screw like pieces of shit now. When I was in prison I used to call them Mr Jones, Mr Hayes: when I was in Swansea Prison, Mr Hayes had medals from the war. This old guy was very understanding – he had been doing the job for a long time and he came down to reception to check you out for body lice and all that and he said, 'Mr Price, do you want to come up to my guard?'

I said, 'Yeah, Mr Hayes.'

I could go and see him any time I wanted to get the job done.

I really respected those people. They only have a job to do, but it was Mr this and Mr that, and at that time I was going to Swansea Prison back and forth like a fiddler's elbow.

I was in Tredegar with Mike Mahoney, Roy Elliott and a few others, and we went to this pub for the first pint, a

Sunday starter. This pub was a well-known haunt for hard men and was a cider house. We went in there and it wasn't a place where men used their fists when they fought, some were tool merchants.

Trouble was brewing. We ordered cider and each of us also ordered a bottle of Double Maxim, and there was a reason for this. We were all now equally tooled up with our bottles on the bar! Before anyone could do anything, we'd battered them with the bottles. The fight continued out into this lane and the police had been called.

Mahoney was shouting at me that he couldn't get away from one of these tool merchants. I looked and the fellow had a hold of Mahoney by his leg. I got hold of the fellow's thumb and snapped it back until the back of his thumb bent back 90 degrees and it was touching the top of his wrist and he soon let go of Mahoney.

So we went off on our way and I said to the boys, 'Come on, let's go somewhere that I'm not known.' As we were walking along, this fellow, who was old to us at about 40 or 50, whacked me over the head with a walking stick! I could hear the thud. It opened my head up like a mackerel and there was blood everywhere. I turned around and battered the old fellow and knocked him out.

Mahoney picked up the stick to break it and there was a great big fucking brass end the size of a door knocker on the end of it! Even though I had a terrible gash in my head, it didn't move me, probably good practice for when I was to get an axe embedded in my head, but that's another story.

My time as a doorman was quite volatile and bloody; no door registration schemes or training courses could have prepared you for what it was like back then. You didn't have vanloads of police patrolling up and down the town then, in fact, you were lucky if you even saw a couple of bobbies in a car, never mind on foot.

I was fitting my door work in with my job at the Heads of the Valley roads, as an earthmoving machine operative, and burning the candle at both ends was no trouble to a young man like I was back then, but I used to burn the candle at both ends and in the middle! It was hard getting up for work in the mornings! I was even involved in a documentary about club doormen once. There weren't any stimulants around then like there are now; it was all to do with will power. How the hell I was doing it all, I'll never know.

The only kicks and highs people got then were the ones dished out in nightclub fights. Perhaps they just wanted to make a name for themselves, I don't know. Then it was just fighting and drinking and fighting and drinking – I'm a man, I can drink and fight, is how it went! Some of them in the nightclubs had too much to drink and when we could handle them we just put them out, but some of the bastards ... they like it; like going to a football match today, they don't go for the sport they just start violence for the sake of it.

I had this gift for a long time. I was pretty good, I could look into a fellow's face and eyes and I could tell; the attitude, he's out for trouble, and I'd say, 'Fucking out.' And you know whether you're going to be able to talk your way out of it or if he was all for it! I used to go in like a fucking bull. The attitude of the man and his eyes would tell you and that was it. I can't tell now, as I have to wear glasses. Some people say you should watch a man's feet to see if he's ready to swing a punch, I say watch his fucking eyes!

My safeguard was to look into his eyes, that was my motto. I'd hit him on the bottom or hit him wherever. Gone was the boxing, that's the thing. When I boxed, I had Eddie Thomas in my mind, and in the boxing ring you can't kick the fellow up the backside. Mind, at times, I was tempted to bring the rough and tumble stuff I'd learned on the earthmoving sites and in the dancehalls into the ring!

I was once hit after the bell. I didn't see it coming, he came in front of me and pushed me back and, as he was pushing me back, I caught one from him! I made a beeline for him and he made a beeline for me, so I kicked him up the arse! Well, the crowd loved that; they had never seen boxing like it, had they. Kicking him up the arse was the first thing that came into my mind on the spur of the moment. It was like a pantomime in the end, and the crowd were roaring. They loved it, they did, and I liked it as well and I couldn't give a fuck.

My pro-boxing career was short lived. I'm not going to say what most failed boxers say: 'I coulda been a contenda.' No! I'm not saying that at all. I had no real boxing ambition and I'm not a liar. I went in to each contest with no big ideas of being the champion, but at times when I was the champion I felt good. Who knows what I could have gone on to. I only mention this as there have been people who said I could have gone all the way, but how many thousands of boxers has that been said about? Only a handful ever make it to greatness.

I'd like to mention some of the men I fought at pro level.

They are: Carlton Prince – my first fight – I knocked him out in the fourth. Cliff Purnell – I stopped him in the fourth. Billy Wynter – I stopped him in the fourth or fifth. Roy Seward – he had a badly cut eye so they stopped the fight in the fourth. I lost twice to fucking big Jim Monaghan. The second time I fought Monaghan; if it had gone another round I would have knocked him out.

Not many people know about Chick Calderwood (light heavyweight), the quiet Scot. He never got to fight in the last fight lined up for him; he was killed in a car crash. He was a contender, but the only time we were head-to-head was when they put me in the ring with him for a sparring session in Ebbw Vale.

I also had a few sparring sessions with the legendary Howard Winstone, the Welsh Wizard (World Featherweight Champion); he hit me seven times before I turned around. He was a much lighter guy; he could hit you, but the impact wouldn't be as hard as a heavyweight could punch, but he was lightning fast. Still, he was a puncher; he was there and then he wasn't, that's how fast he was. He was like a dancer; he could balance and spin a man around and next thing he'd have him on the ropes.

Oh, yes, he was marvellous. I come from the same town as him, so he was in the same gym. It was the same with all the boys in the gym; they were all pros and champions as well. Sadly, Howard died in October 2000.

I only ever had the support of my father once or twice, when he came to watch me box when there were pros there. He came to one or two amateur fights with his mates and he came to one fight when I was a professional in Ebbw Vale, when I fought Roy Seward. I didn't even know my father was there, as I hadn't invited him.

My boxing career lay in tatters; I had to get on with my life … but not quietly! Faced with having to earn an income from other sources, I soon became the top troubleshooter for pubs and clubs in the Welsh Valleys. I also turned my hand to a bit of debt collecting on the side. This boosted my income beyond what I would have earned as an up-and-coming pro boxer. Although boxing had turned its back on me, I wasn't finished as a fighter.

CHAPTER 4

FIGHTING TOWN

Name: Tydfil. Derived from: a Welsh Christian princess martyred by pagan invaders. The name given to the Welsh settlement was derived from the martyr, St Tydfil – Merthyr Tydfil. So that's the romantic notion out of the way!

Merthyr, in modern times, is, you could say, a fighting town. There were a lot of hard nuts around, old legends, starting with the likes of Redmond Coleman who was around in the late 1800s up until he passed away in the 1920s. They could use their fucking hands, and they did boxing and they were street fighters at the same time, but this was nearly a hundred years ago.

Then there was the likes of old Freddy Reagan who was good with his head and all that. He broke people's jaws with one butt of his head. He was a right proper handful in his time, the typical flat-nosed street fighter, weighing about 15 stone and about 5 ft 7in tall. He used to walk around the town with two or three Alsatians; everybody was terrified of him in his day.

I remember this time in the Beehive pub, when I said to Freddy, 'Hey, fancy your chances?'

Freddy replied, 'Malcolm, I'm 42 years of age; I've got no chance with you. I'm finished now. I'd like to have had a go at you a few years ago, but I'm finished now. It wouldn't last a minute.'

I left it at that. I wasn't going to take liberties, and I was far younger, fitter, faster and harder than this old street fighter.

And then there was the likes of Di Davies, Di Mathews and Billy Eynon, and a lot more. Mind you, there was a lot of shit around at the time as well. I was fighting a lot, I had a bit of a reputation and people would come up to me and wind me up by saying, 'Di Davies is coming up,' and this sort of shit was stirring it for me.

This man, Di Davies, was a good looker: he had all his own teeth, fucking beautiful white pearly whites at that, and he could pull the ladies a bit as well. Most of the time, Di was in prison. One time, though, when he was fresh out of prison, somebody introduced me to him.

He replied in a gruff voice, 'So! You're the middle heavyweight boxer, like.'

I cautiously said, 'Aye.'

My mind should have been stirred by his expression and his stirred by mine. Hard man meets hard man type of thing!

I was told by those in awe of him, 'You just had to blink your eyes at him and you'd be on the fucking floor.' He had the reputation of putting five policemen out at a time, and that was just with his head! He was really fucking good, so they reckoned. Mind you, I'd never come across this man before because he was always in prison.

A while after we were introduced, it happened in the Swan pub. I walked in the Swan one night and he was there. People used to buy him drinks all night. That night, when he left the pub he tried to put the head in on some poor fucker. Mahoney grabbed a hold of him and they both fell on to the ground. That was a trick, you know, just stick the fucking head in to some unsuspecting fucker for the sake of it.

Through the darkness, I could see the shadowy figure of Davies lurking in a doorway; he was peering out ready to pounce on some unsuspecting victim. The other boys didn't see him and so they went on by and into the pub. I held back and I walked up and, anyway, all the boys had gone for a singsong. Tonight, Davies was going to get some of the Pricey treatment – a one-way ticket to the hospital!

It was a Friday night and I said, 'I can fucking see you there, so where you at, like?'

He said, 'What's the marrer, man, what's the marrer?'

I said, 'You're a dirty bastard, you shouldn't have done what you done.'

He tried to creep closer and that was fatal for head butting!

I said, 'Don't come anywhere near me, just stand where you fucking are!'

He said, 'Fuck you!'

So this was it! I gave him a good fucking kicking; he was trying to get at me all the time, to grab hold of me so as to lay the head in. I had a good laugh at banging his fucking head.

I had a six-inch nail in my pocket and why I used it I'll never know, because I don't use such things. I thrust my arm at him and my fist that was holding the nail went crashing into the side of his head! A spurt of blood pumped out into the night air. You could smell it – there was dark, greasy blood everywhere. The nail I had plunged into his head had caused the hole where the blood was gushing out. I chucked the nail away.

He said, 'You dirty bastard!'

So, then, I gave him a straight right, which knocked him clean out and I then set about putting the boot in and I thought, you're not going to get up from this. Then, the police came and I stood back and there was a big crowd around by this time. Davies was saturated in his own blood.

I heard the police say to him, 'Who done this to you?'

I said, 'Fuck off.'

The police said, 'Who done this to you, Davies?'

Davies collected a mouthful of blood and he spat it all over the fucking police. He was a hard boy; he was old school. I admired him for that. I waited until all had dispersed, and he got up and sat on the windowsill of this shop where it had happened.

There was a lot of blood on the floor and I went up to him and said, 'Davies!'

He said, 'Who is it?'

I said, 'Pricey.'

'Ah fuck,' he said.

I said, 'Come on, I'll take you up to the hospital.'

'Will you fuck! Fuck off and leave me alone,' was his reply.

I said, 'You're bleeding badly. I think it could need stitches.'

He repeated what he'd already told me, 'Just fuck off!'

I admired him for what he done. There were a lot of rumours about him going to look for me, and Mahoney said, 'I don't think you should look for him.' Di Davies and me have become fucking good friends now. He wasn't a working boy like me; he used to be around the place, in Swansea living with a piece down there or in Caerphilly! He's been all over South Wales.

Every time I'd see him, I'd always tip him a few quid or, if he was in the Iron Horse or wherever, and if I ever saw him on the street, I'd say, 'Are you coming in for a pint?' We'd always have a pint together. They were terrified of him; I can be honest about that. Lots of these so-called fucking hard blokes, they would shake if he walked into the pub, they would fucking shake and fuck off.

After that, he was obviously still using the head butt tactics and whenever you went down, he'd put the fucking boot into you, so you had to make sure he didn't get back up. I learned that very quickly. As soon as you put them down, you kept them down! There was no giving them a count of 'eight' and letting them get back up on their feet, no way!

Although there have been one or two scary moments, I haven't actually shit myself, but I've been worried about one or two of them that I've put out cold. I'd hear that so-and-so's in a bad way, like, from the police, and I'd say, 'Fucking hell, he's not that bad, is he? Will he pull through?' These things just don't come into your head during the course of a set-to, but afterwards you hope the bloke's strong enough to pull through.

There were times when violence never came into it; just the mere threat of what I could do would be sufficient to quell any trouble. One such situation arose at the local Chinese takeaway. There was four or five of these fuckers and they were nibbling at me. I was on my own and I forget the exact words that he said, but he more or less fucking insulted me.

I said, 'Don't you worry, there's plenty of time, I'll see you outside after.' They all laughed. When I went outside, I just took my coat off and said, 'There's you and me.' I wouldn't back down; I just couldn't back down in those days.

I knew what I fucking knew, 'If I catch one of you then you'll go down, but if I go down then it's fair enough ...'

That was it. It never came to anything, and they all went this way and that and I said, 'Come on then,' and they all stepped back. There was no fear. No, there was no fear.

The third time I had a run-in with the police, it was a fucking sham. They sent a policewoman and two policemen. I was fighting with three boys outside my house and I was living beside my gran's fruit shop at that time, right at the beginning of the town. This policewoman and two policemen came on the scene. The policewoman grabbed hold of me and these other fuckers I'd been fighting with were still throwing punches at me. I said to the policewoman, 'Get off me and let me do my thing.'

You never hold a person when they're fighting. You get one or two in and, fuck me, they're holding you, and I just pushed her out of the way like that and I said, 'Fuck off, they're trying to hit me, man!'

Then I was the one who was booked for assault and, out

of frustration, I smashed this fellow's glasses, chucked them on the road and I started fucking into them again. The three of them had the fucking cheek to book me in for assault and, furthermore, a policewoman tried to have me for assault.

Well, Eddie Thomas said, 'If he had assaulted you then he would have knocked your fucking head off.' That's what he said to the policewoman. I called Eddie Thomas as a witness, and he said, 'You should never hold people that are fighting. Where was the two other fucking idiots?' meaning the other two policemen.

That was early on in my fighting life, but it was my third run-in with the police. The old police force would say, 'Put him in the fucking cells.' I knew half of them because they knew my father. I'd never done big time because there was a lot of people on the bench and they knew I was an ex-choirboy, and there was a lot of good in me, not all fucking bad.

I can't deny that I was lucky through life. It's as if someone up there likes me. Little stupid things I can remember about the fairness of the majority of the police in Merthyr came through in the way some of them handled situations. One day, they caught me pissing. All right, I was taken short, I couldn't make it to the watershed because I was busy talking and we were having a good crack, and they came over because the copper could see the water trickling down.

One of the old-time policemen, a sergeant, said, 'Hello, hello, Price.'

'I'm awfully sorry,' I said, 'but I was taken short.'

'Well, we'll leave it this time; make sure you make the toilet the next time round, my friend,' he said.

But, just as I was making some headway with my relations with the local police, there would always be one who had to be a funny cunt. Once I was talking to some fellow and the boys went on to town, where they were going to the nightclub. There was a pedestrian crossing just by the New Inn, in the centre of town. I was finishing talking to this fellow and I went to run across the crossing when a police car came down. I wasn't really drunk, I was tight but I wasn't drunk and I was shouting: 'Yeehaaaaa … I've got to catch up to the boys.'

The policeman shouted, 'Whoa, whoa! You're drunk.'

I said, 'You were coming down too fast, I'm not drunk.'

He said, 'You're coming down to the police station and I'm booking you for being drunk and disorderly.'

I wasn't drunk and disorderly, I was sober. I said, 'You're at me for nothing. This is for nothing at all.'

He replied, 'You're coming down the police station, now!'

I said, 'Why don't you just take your coat off, there's a lane up there, why don't we go and sort it out like two men, because you're picking on me.'

Anyway, I went down that alley and got booked for being drunk and disorderly.

The Swan pub was a regular trouble spot. There was this big Irish boy who come into town who was living in the Swan. A tough old bugger, he was knocking all the other Irish boys about. He was a big blond lump of a boy. Blondie, we used to call him. Amongst his fellow Irishmen,

Blondie was well known. He used to travel the country as a labourer, a good working man.

This particular night, I was in the Swan with Mike Mahoney and I noticed once more that Blondie was throwing his weight around. I'd had enough of him bullying smaller men so I set about him. The walls of the bar were awash with his blood and he ended up with a face like a squashed tomato. He was another ambulance case.

The next morning, I went for a pint and I was told that Blondie was in a bad way. I'd given him a broken nose, broken cheekbone, and this, that and the other! About two weeks later, Blondie came out of hospital and he said, 'I'll never put my hands up in this town again, thanks to that Malcolm Price.' So there was another bully put paid to.

Another time, up in the Tiger bar in Merthyr (they called it the Imperial but we used to call it the Tiger bar), this fellow called Des had had a bit of a mental turn. He was a big lump of a man and he was going around, downing a few pints and challenging people out, and, fair play to him, he was battering most of them and doing the business on them because he was going a bit mad.

Most of the pubs had barred Des, but he came into the Tiger bar and he pointed to me and said, 'And you, out! I want you by the back of the car park.' So I obliged him and proceeded to kick the poor cunt all around the car park; he ended up in hospital for a week! Eventually, when he came out of hospital, he said that I was the best thing that had happened to him; I'd cured him! He never challenged anyone again. What the doctors couldn't do, I did! How I never did big time in prison, I'll never know.

Looking back on it, I was as mad as this man I'd booted about the car park.

At that time, there was only one thing better than a good fight, and that was having a good fight and getting paid for it. In my bouncing days, there was a dance going down at George Town and Elwyn Morgan was running this dance at the time. He used to do a lot of organising of dances and things and I used to do a lot of bouncing for him. I remember this night because we had to stop the dance because the place was chock-a-block.

Although we didn't have a specific head-count limit, we knew when the place was packed like a sardine can and, for safety reasons, we had to limit the amount of people that were teeming in.

I remember this particular night, the dance hall kicked off and just about everyone was fighting, even the women were fighting! Eventually, we got them all stuffed out of the doors. We stuck them out in the courtyard and, by this time, somebody must have phoned for the police and everything. The courtyard was out in the main road. That was hard work; you were frightened of the amplifiers and everything getting damaged.

The punters had become angry and started to turn police cars over and I saw three boys in front of this policeman; he must have been one of the first policemen to arrive on the Wild West scene. These three boys were kicking three colours of shite out of this copper and he was bleeding pretty bad and he was right out of it, and if they had put many more boots in to his head then they would have killed him. I more or less saved a man's frigging life. I wasn't interested in seeing a man die in such a way ... he probably had a wife and kids at home.

I was chucking these punters off the policeman and shouting, 'He's had enough, man; he's out of it!' So, although I had run-ins with the police from time to time, I saved that policeman. By this time the police were getting the crowd in order by using their truncheons.

Later, I saw the rest of the policemen and they were chucking the riotous mob into the meat wagons like fucking wild animals off for the slaughter. There was about 18 or 20 coppers chucking the rowdy mob in and, if they had got them all, they couldn't have locked them up, because they wouldn't have had the space.

Obviously it's hard for anyone to imagine, but these dance halls were powder kegs just waiting to explode. Names were made and reputations were enhanced or blown in a flash! I would stand at the back of the hall patiently watching for troublemakers. The instant any trouble started, I'd put my glass down, walk over and sort it and usually that was the end of it.

Nightclub skirmishes were easy to handle, but there were times that the odd skirmish would take place with the local hard cases and that needed a little more than this sort of intervention.

One such man went by the name of Mervyn the Black. He used to work over in Aberdare, and had a steel plate in his head! A friend of mine, little Geoff Fenerollie, had problems over there with Mervyn the Black, the top lad over in Aberdare at that time.

Little Geoff said, 'I'm going to sort him out.' He's a good

little boxer is Geoff; he also worked for Wimpy sometimes. I did him a favour when he asked me to watch his back in an organised fight he was to have with Mervyn the Black.

He said, 'Pricey, there may be more than one with this fucker and I want to have a go myself.'

I said, 'From what I know of this Mervyn the Black, you're giving a bit of weight away here.' I just said it like that.

Geoff said, 'Would you come across and see that nothing dodgy goes on?'

I replied, 'Yes, what do you want me to do?'

'I just want you to come across and see that there's fair play,' he said.

I said, 'That's fair, man.'

This fight was to take place just outside of Aberdare. I took big Lyn Richards along; I used to do a lot of bouncing with big Lyn.

We got to the place, went in and locked the door behind us. I had said to lock the door on the man and then 'you have a go, man to man'.

Geoff said, 'What if anyone's around?'

I told him, 'Don't worry, if anyone's around, I'll give him a slap and me and big Lyn will see that it's a one-to-one.'

Anyway, Mervyn the Black was too big and powerful for Geoff. The fight started with Geoff using his fists, and if it had stayed that way then it would have gone Geoff's way, but it was to go down on the floor now and Mervyn was kneeling on Geoff and killing him.

I said, 'That's fucking it now, sound. You're too powerful for him.' So it was left at that and the police were forgotten about and we got in the car and went for a drink.

I've been inside with a lot of boys from Aberdare down in Swansea. Aberdare has a name in the rugby fraternity; you stop over there and that's when things seem to blow up.

I was down in Ystalyfera one night and the club boss said, 'Will you come back down?'

I said, 'Oh, aye,' because Danny Sullivan was there and he used to do a lot of bouncing as well when we were younger. I took the work down there to help him out a bit.

I said, 'There are a lot of fellows down here, good 'uns, they're from Swansea and they'll see you all right.' He offered me more money, though, so I took it and said, 'All right.'

'I want you, I don't want anyone from nearby, I want you,' he said.

I said, 'All right.'

I wondered how he got in to so much trouble in this pub here. The footballing brothers John and Mel Charles are well known in Wales. I met Mel Charles down there and we got really friendly with him through me doing the bouncing.

Anyway, I didn't go down to Ystalyfera for a week or two. I couldn't get down for a fortnight and he couldn't make the club work or something. This Mel Charles used to bring coach loads from down in Swansea and everywhere, but it didn't take off; it just wasn't in the right place. I think being opposite the police station could've been something to do with that!

I went back down and the troublemakers had bitten one of the bouncer's fingers through. They said to Sullivan the bouncer, 'Where's that big blond bastard?' The big blond bastard? Well, that was me.

When I got there, Sullivan said, 'There was about six or eight of them, Price, and they were going to wreck the fucking place, so I had to shut the door on them.'

So I went back down again to ensure there was no further trouble at the club. Well, of course, there was no trouble when I was there, so I thought I'd go out myself and look for the troublemakers because there were a few other pubs and clubs around there.

I went looking for these bastards and I took a few extra boys with me. One was Peter Morgan, who used to run the Wyndum pub in Merthyr with his brother, Di. Peter could use himself; he was a big rugby boy. We were all brought up together in Gurnos at Merthyr Tydfil. The Morgans were living right opposite my father; they were a big family. Di was nicknamed 'The Gurnos Strangler'.

Peter was a good rugby player and he's well to do in the rugby circles now, and he does things for charity on these big walks. He piled on a lot of weight, hell of a boy; he's good company Peter and so is Di. He's put on a lot of weight, too. I offered him this American diet so he could lose a stone, but in one week he was back on his usual intake of food and drink.

Anyway, back to the story. I also took big Casey. He's about 30-something fucking stone, he is. He used to bounce years ago when I was at the Sands. I couldn't find any of those fucking troublemakers anywhere and if they were in the pub they should have stood up.

In one club, a social club, I was in the bar and said, 'I'm

looking for someone, I wonder if you can help me? There has been a few local boys going into the nightclub down the road who have been causing hell.'

'We don't get anybody in here like that but you might try the pubs around,' came the reply.

I said, 'I've tried them. I walked in and nobody stood up.'

'I can't help you,' the landlord said. So that was the end of that.

When this sort of trouble happened, your adrenaline glands would be pumping and you would be primed and ready. But there were times when you ended up going round in circles trying to track down the troublemakers. There were other times when a potential situation turned into a comedy, instead of violence.

One night I was in the local Indian restaurant and an incident happened that was so comical that I nearly burst a rib with laughing. You don't expect to get trouble from people who want you as a customer, but that's what happened here. I was with a friend of mine, little Mel, and decided to make a call on this new Indian that hadn't been long in town. Eventually, after a lengthy wait, they put the food out. I never take the piss out of anyone, not until this night. When it came, the food was cold; it wasn't even lukewarm.

I said, 'This food is cold and I'm not eating it!'

Mel said, 'I'm not fucking eating it either, it's fucking cold, Price.'

I said, 'We're not eating this and we're not paying for it!'

I walked out of the place, and these little Indian fellows tried to pull me back in, and that was when one of the Indians went for a short journey ... over the table!

The next thing, the police were there. The thing is, such a matter relating to food is civil, and the police can do fuck all when it's a genuine case of a meal being rejected. We hadn't even eaten any of it!

The Indians told us to get back in there and finish the meal and I told the Indians, 'But the fucking food is cold! Get back in there yourselves, you little bastards!'

When the police came in, they didn't book me. The policeman pointed at one of the Indians and said, 'He said you pushed him?' It was like a Laurel and Hardy movie!

I said, 'I'm not paying for cold food.'

I'd never had any trouble paying in other Indians all the other times and the sergeant said, 'No, you haven't, Price. I'll give you your due.'

You know why he said that? Because he thought it was hilarious, because he saw me pushing these little Indians back in and it was like punching fresh air. Even the policeman burst out laughing at the farcical situation. I mean, this wasn't a racist thing; in fact, racism hadn't even been invented then!

One of the Indians said that I had knocked the table down as well. He said, 'You tried to kill my heart,' and we all burst out laughing. Such an incident caused all of Merthyr to laugh at the exaggerated claims of these Indians.

The very next day, the Indian incident forgotten, Mike, Colin and me were down at Quakers Yard, in Merthyr. We went over to see Terry Cardiff, we had a few pints and the crack was good.

In the pub, someone mouthed off to Colin and Colin said, 'Come outside.' I thought, Here it is again! So he started fighting outside, and two of the other guy's mates went outside after them.

I said, 'It's only one-to-one here.'

So they turned around and started flinging punches and the three of them were left on the floor. We put the boots in and flattened them and that was the end of that one.

Someone, as usual, must have called the police when we were outside of the pub, so we darted round the corner and left these three hospital cases lying on the floor. Old Barney had seen the police car come around that way so we started walking because there was no one else watching. When we got around the corner we said, 'We haven't got a vehicle, we haven't phoned a taxi or nothing!'

A big Irishman came up and said, 'Come in here, lads,' and he took us into the living quarters of the chip shop and that's where we stayed in hiding.

I could hear the police outside saying, 'Did you see anything?' Luckily for us, we must have ducked down in the alleyway just before the police van passed. Barney the Irishman had us a taxi home and we were safe! God bless the Irish!

You would think that all fights start with people mouthing it off, but there are times when someone's actions can be just as volatile as someone mouthing it off. There was a big fellow keeping the New Inn in Merthyr, which was situated on a corner. In the pub were Roy Evans, and his brother, Les Evans – he was a smart boy, who was wearing a nice suit. The big new fellow had a dog behind the bar – it was a Doberman, and a nasty bastard.

I think it was on a Saturday afternoon, and there was

these boys and me and Les. We were talking and this and that, having a good old chat, when we saw a fellow coming up from behind Les's back. He had a bag on his shoulder and I didn't know the fellow. I had never seen this fellow before and d'you know what he was doing? He was burning a hole in Les's coat from the back! I said, 'Hey!' Les didn't know what was happening, he was just going to walk out, so I grabbed hold of the fellow and I threw him over the bar and table. The landlord hadn't seen what had happened and, when he came over, he said, 'No trouble in here.' He then told us, the innocent party, to get out.

The hole-burner fellow was on the floor soon enough, where I had put him. As this fellow came from behind the bar, I tipped a chair over and ripped the leg off and said, 'I don't want to hurt you or your fucking dog, so keep him on the leash. I don't like hurting animals.'

The landlord said, 'Well, get out now before I phone for the police.'

I said, 'That's fair enough and as long as you don't get in my fucking way.' As I had a chair leg in my hand, he had no choice but to stand aside and let me go.

The following morning, somebody must have told the police where I was. It's surprising, but I was seeing my mother and father at the time. I was between motorway jobs and hardly anybody knew I was back ... but word soon spread. Anybody who was put in hospital from outside of the town, it was me they'd look for. They'd say: 'Where were you last night, Price?'

But they would always come to my house and my old man, he asked me once, 'Did you put this fellow in hospital?'

I said, 'You stay in there, Mam, I don't want you to speak to the police.'

So the old man went to the door and came back and said, 'Did you do anything wrong last night, there's two policemen here at the door?'

I said, 'No.'

So he went back to the door and said, 'Fuck off from my door,' and it went no further. I've got to give him credit for that, but was it just so he didn't have the police at his door or was it for my benefit? I'll never know.

I swear, if there's a pub full of happy people then one bastard has to come along and try and spoil it for them. This was the case when my friend Gerald Morgan and me were in the Tydfil Arms in Merthyr on a Saturday afternoon. We returned there for a second session on the Saturday night and there was a great singsong going on.

Gerald loves the old singsongs, as I do too. Gerald and I were singing along like two canaries, but there was this fellow in there that stood out like a sore thumb. I could see he was intent on causing trouble and the place was packed with people wall-to-wall. There wasn't any trouble; except for this guy, everyone was having a great night.

Gerald could see what this fellow was up to.

I shouted over the top of the singing to Gerald, 'I'll not cause trouble, I'll wait 'til he goes for a piss and then I'll go and see him in the toilet.'

Gerald winked acknowledgement at what I'd said and shouted back, 'I can see what's going on, Price, if he keeps on I'll give him a bang myself.'

I beat Gerald to it. When he went on the microphone

singing, the fellow went to the toilet and I was in tow right behind him. When I went in the toilet, there were two fellows in there having a talk, and I start talking to this nuisance maker.

I said, 'You're a fucking nuisance, why are you causing trouble when everybody's fucking happy?'

'I'm doing fuck all,' he replied.

With that, I knocked him out like a fucking light. And the other two fellows shot out through the door and I left the lousy good-for-nothing troublemaker lying there.

The ambulance came and took him away, I thought that was the end of that. The next morning, I didn't think any more about it. It was Sunday morning and I was preparing to go out for another session. I was with another character from Merthyr who's a good crack, Donald McCarthy, and we called up to Gerald Morgan's to go out for a drink. I knocked on the door and Gerald's wife, Lil, answered.

'Come in, Don and Pricey, he's just getting ready.'

I shouted up the stairs, 'Come on, Morgan, we'll be late for the pub.'

Lil put the kettle on and asked, 'Cup of tea, Pricey?'

Don and me both said, 'Yes.'

Lil went on to say, 'You had a good night then, last night?'

'Yes, Lil,' I replied, just assuming she was making small talk.

She said, 'Did you hear about some feller having to be taken out of the Tydfil Arms by ambulance last night?'

I calmly hid my surprise and replied in a normal tone of voice, 'No, Lil.'

She said, 'Well, we heard that he died in hospital last night!'

My calmness had vanished as I spilled the cup of tea all over the carpet and, with shock in my voice, I said, 'Fucking hell, is that right?'

My whole life had been turned upside down. I could already hear the judge saying, 'Price, I have no alternative but to give you a life sentence. Take him down!'

Just as I was coming to terms with what Lil had said, Morgan came down from upstairs and burst out laughing!

'You pair of bastards,' I said, as I sighed a breath of relief in the knowledge that I wouldn't be facing a murder charge. Morgan's laughter was my reprieve. The thing is, Lil was so serious when she was saying it. Gerald had told Lil to set me up; a crazy pair with a wicked sense of humour.

After that shock, we couldn't wait to get over to the pub to have another drink to get over the shock, Donald and me. I was already feeling the worse for wear from the drink I'd had the night before and, like they say, a bit of the hair of the dog that bit you …

Although Morgan and Lil had been pulling my leg about this man that had supposedly died in hospital, this next incident was far more sinister. That day, I was out with big Mickey Mochan; we'd been down to see a mate of mine, McLarfety, at a place called Llantrisant.

The day had been a long one; we were hungry and night was setting in. We stopped outside this chip shop at Talbot Green on the way from Llantrisant and all the people were screaming because these no-good arseholes on trials bikes were riding along on the path, causing mayhem with their stunt riding. These people who were screaming were terrified; they were afraid to go on the path.

I'd just come on to the scene after they'd been racing on the footpath. They had continued on for a while, but I could see that there was one or two of the motorbikes making a u-turn and heading back towards us. Suddenly, out of what seemed like nowhere, one of the motorbikes was coming straight for me at a ripe old speed! I thought, fuck this!

Mickey bawled, 'Stand back, Price.'

I said, 'Fuck him!'

As one of the motorbikes came towards me, I let a big heavy right go, and knocked the rider's head clean off his shoulders! Fucking hell, the guy's head was still in his helmet and it was clattering all the way down the road!

It was dark but, as the motorbike sped away, all that I could see was the silhouette of a headless rider and – what must have obviously been a reflex action – his hands were still holding on to the handlebars of the motorbike! I thought, fuck me, I've knocked his fucking head off here!

Mickey come over to me and said, 'Fucking hell, you've done it now, Price! You've decapitated him!' We tentatively walked over to where the helmet had stopped rolling and expected to see the gory mess of veins, sinews and arteries hanging out.

I was still furious at the bikers and I kicked the helmet … it was empty! Obviously the rider had rode off with his head pulled down, making me believe the worse. Everybody in Talbot Green was happy because the motorbikes had all fucked off, but no one was more happy than me!

These near-death escapades didn't put me off working in violent situations. If trouble started, I couldn't stop to think of what might happen. There were some good people about and my job was to protect them from trouble. I couldn't let past experiences put me off.

The Buffalo pub in Merthyr used to be run by Malcolm and Mary. They were some of the nicest people – genuine – I had plenty of time for them. They used to offer me food, and we went there for dinner one time and there were candles set out on the table and everything.

Malcolm and Mary's daughter was married to Paddy, and they had a full pub every night and I used to watch the door for them. When trouble happened and I was laying down the law and going hell for leather with some troublemaker, Malcolm would say, 'That's enough, Price.' That was all he had to say. Normally, I was like a bull when I started but I had respect for Malcolm and that's what I was paying him back with when I listened to him. They're living down West now, Malcolm and Mary, and their son's a policeman, he was a good character.

As much as Merthyr is a fighting town, these people also have a heart of gold. I worked all over Monmouth, and then the Aberfan disaster happened. That was a very emotional episode in my life. I never want to see anything like that ever again. In my opinion, the tip should have been moved well before the rain got in to it, because when it came rolling down the hillside on to the school, the walls just caved in!

They sent for all the trucks in the area because the place was a panic station. This was on the Friday, and on the wireless they said that some kid had slid and knocked the wall down, but it wasn't that. The slurry from the tip was what had engulfed the school in a sludge of death. The poor kids and everybody that was down there at that time didn't stand a chance.

I didn't want to see ... they had to stop the trucks and they had the machinery then and they were catching the bodies ... no, it wasn't nice to see at all. You had to stop the trucks and take things out of the back and I never want to see anything like that again. I was involved in helping clearing the debris away from the school and it was terrible, terrible, terrible! I was down there, and I saw miners digging with their bare hands. Obviously that was a Welsh tragedy that will never be forgotten, but to have it happen to children, it was a terrible thing, terrible!

When such a tragedy happens, you see how much fight a person has in them and that's when Merthyr became a fighting town with a difference. Instead of fighting each other, they were fighting to save lives and I shared in some of that emotion. Such tragedies hammer home how frail we all are. As tough as a man is on the outside, on the inside he's only human. But, although I had compassion for what happened, it didn't stop me fighting.

One night, not long after that, I was in George Town. The landlord was Glynn Davis, but we just called him Glynn Shag. That night, I was fighting, and there was about four of the bastards after me. I remember how it started. I went to the toilet and one or two followed me in. I turned fast from the hip and belted one of them, but I didn't catch him properly and he was holding out, so I grabbed hold of the other one and I had him in a headlock, ran with him to a cubicle and put his head down the shithouse. I was cracking his head off the toilet bowl; how that pan didn't break I'll never know.

Although the pan didn't break, it certainly could cut and I was working away on his head. I think I was a bit rough and, as I was hammering his head on the back of the pan, I had to flush the blood away because there was so much of it. When I finished with him, the shithouse floor was like an abattoir!

The trouble had started when the drummer in the band playing on stage went to the bar to get some beers in. I took over the drums for a while. Some of the lads were taking the piss out of my drumming technique. This went on for a while, until my patience snapped and the red mist came down on me and all hell broke loose.

There were three or four on the floor. I got to know this Scots fellow really well; he was younger than me, a hell of a nice fellow and a big strong lad. He used to work for Jim Russell; Jim had the contract in for the steel fixing. He used to bend the steel for the bridges ... not with his bare hands though!

Even though Merthyr was a fighting town, it still had some old worldly charm pubs. I remember when I first went into the Express pub, there was an old couple keeping it and there was never any trouble in there. The landlord was Mr Lloyd and they used to call him Lloydy; he was in with all the toffs in the back room. That was their room.

As for the bar, it was a cider house and they were very

fussy about who they let in. There was never any trouble in there because it was always old people who used to frequent the place for the cider, and they were well respected. They used to put roast tatties on the stove for the old people and they could help themselves to pepper and salt. They looked after the customers, never mind how old they were.

There used to be one fellow who got in there, who was a nasty-looking old parcel. He wore his cap pulled down all the time. Every night, him and his dog were in. They all had their regular places, no matter how full it was, the seats were always left for the old wives.

One night, they bet me that I wouldn't sit in this particular regular's seat; and he was due in any moment.

I said, 'I will.'

I was told, 'I bet he tells you to "fuck off out of the seat".'

I said, 'No! I don't think so.'

So they put me to the test, see, and we had a bet over it, a couple of fellows and me. Anyway, in he strolls with his dog and the first thing he sees is me sitting in the prized seat with a pint and we were bent over it, me and a couple of fellows.

I saw him coming in and quickly looked away. He didn't say anything, he went straight up to the bar and Lloydy was laughing. The thing is, the old geezer turned it on, put his pint on the table, took his stick off his hand and cracked me over the head with it and told me to 'Fuck off'. To him, it didn't matter that I was Price. I liked that.

I used to like the old fellows; they trusted us and we

trusted them. When I was working, I used to go in at Christmas time, and say, 'A pint for all the old ages,' and there were mostly old ages in the pub! But they were all characters and it was an expensive round, but at the time it was only nine pence a pint. There were a few oddballs who got in to the pub and they would say, 'Does that include me, Price?'

I'd say, 'No, it does not, this is for the old age.'

When I first went in there, I was with Ginger Harris, who's older than me. The first time you went in there, you weren't allowed to drink rough cider. Anybody going in there for the first time wasn't; you had to go for four to six weeks on trial! You had to drink beer whether you liked it or not. The cider was out of the barrel.

After my probationary period, I succeeded in getting my first real pint. We got to know the landlady really well and I used to go in there regularly and she would say, 'Have you had food, Mal? Come here.' She always had her dog in the bar. She would comb him and brush him, very fussy you know, she used to go in the back and check herself in the mirror quite often.

Old people are in a different world. When they used to tell me to 'stay back, she doesn't want to talk to you.' I used to stay back. I thought you couldn't have it much better. Back then, it was usually a case of your reputation going before you, but they didn't give a shit about any reputation.

The landlord was a very open-minded man and if he didn't like you in the pub he would tell you and you would be straight out on your ear. But whether we were there or not, he was a very straight person and so was his wife, and everyone respected him for what he was. The thing is, he died when I was away, at the time when my mother got taken into hospital.

I was up the General Hospital and there was this little old lady in the opposite bed to my mother, and she always smiled at me every time I went in. I said, 'That lady is always smiling at me, Mam.' I should have known the face: I used to take the daily papers and that. I wondered if she was a regular in the bar. It turned out that she was the landlady, but I didn't recognise her and, when I told the boys, they all went up to see her ... I thought I knew the face.

Although the Express pub was virtually trouble free, and I respected that, there were times when drinking led to trouble. We once got escorted out of the Brecon. We went for a drink, Eddy Lewis and me, and we ended up with a nice gentlemen's day out and we landed up in Brecon, and who was in Brecon at the same time? Big Ken Morgan, who used to train with me when we were inside, and Tashy, an ex-pro fighter, who used to be a good fighter, was with him. Well, they were all looking for fun, see, and they had a showground there at Brecon.

Tashy said to Eddy Lewis, 'How can we knock this showground off and stop it running?' What he wanted to do was to cut all the power off from the generator to the rides and things. 'All the dodgems and everything and all the merry-go-rounds.' They had found the main switch and threw it to the 'off' position, and all the music slowed down and the rides came to a slow standstill!

Well, next thing, all the showmen came out at us with iron bars! There were fucking blue murders there that day and the showmen got a hammering and all ended up on the fucking floor. The boys were taking the bars off the showmen and fucking head butting them in to the next week.

The police couldn't handle it in Brecon. They said that they had another lot of trouble at another function and most of the other police were out of town. One of the policeman said, 'Who's the oldest out of you fucking lot to do the talking?'

I said, 'I'm the father of the team, I'm the oldest.'

'He said, 'Go down there into that pub.'

We went into the pub and the constable and the sergeant came in to speak with us.

The sergeant said, 'We can't fucking handle this because we haven't got enough on the force to see to you fellows. If you jump in the cars now, we'll book you for drink driving and all fucking sorts! But, if you get into those fucking cars and promise to leave Brecon and keep on fucking going, we'll leave you go.'

That's what we did. The police car escorted us right through the lights and turned off and left us to carry on to Merthyr so as to get us out of town.

It was easier to get rid of us by doing that. Little Shorty was laughing and all of the boys had yellow paint all over them because Little Shorty had thrown a bucket of yellow paint through the bastard window, hadn't he? The bar window, it was, and the police manhandled him inside a cell but, luckily, one of the boys had enough money to bail him out.

I said to the police, 'I'm not fucking leaving this town without him. We all came here together and we all go together out of town. Is that fair enough for you?'

The policeman said, 'Lead him out; he's got the money to buy his bail, pay his bail.' We all left together.

There were times that drink had nothing to do with the trouble I found myself in. There was a fellow came up to me one day, but I didn't know him so he must have been from out of town.

This fellow looked like trouble and he said, 'They tell me you're good with your hands?'

I said, 'So what, like?'

I thought, he's trouble: so I butted him out cold and I looked down at him and said, 'I can use my head as well!'

Although I had committed just about every sort of assault imaginable on people and even the odd one or two against the police, I still had – and still do have – respect for the Old School policeman.

Another policeman, Sergeant Graham Miles, is a good mate of mine; he used to open the door of the cell I was in and have a chat: 'What have you done now, Price?' Aye, he let me out a few times. A genuine good fellow and a good fighter himself. But, mind, just because I mention my friendships with these men, it didn't mean I was spilling the beans on what was going on in the criminal underworld.

Remember, I was only into fighting; I wasn't a high-ranking underworld figure selling the Crown Jewels! I wasn't the Merthyr Mafia and I had no connections with the goings on of petty criminal matters. I was only concerned with matters of violence, and any burglar knew to steer well clear of me otherwise I would offer them violence.

I used to bounce for the Labour Club as well. I was in the Labour Club one day and I always helped them out on a Tuesday and Thursday when I was home. Tommy the Greek, he's a comical little fucker; Tommy and me would work the doors together.

Youngsters used to work behind the bar and that day a young boy was behind the bar and there was only a few customers left, as it was close to closing time. My mate's mam was in the bar collecting the glasses and getting the tables ready for the night session. She was mopping out and all that and I said to her, 'I'd better move.'

She said, 'Don't worry about it, I've got the top end to do first.'

So the little kid came out from behind the bar and he was collecting the glasses and tidying up the ashtrays. The kid and I would have a bit of a frisk; he used to have a little fun larking about with a make-believe sparring session with me. I said, 'Come on, you,' and was messing about with the kid. There was three punters sat together. One of them spoke and reckoned he was at school with me.

I said, 'I can't remember you at my school. Which school was that then?'

He replied, 'Pontmorlais.'

I said, 'Fucking hell, that was when we were babies, like.'

'Well,' he said, 'I could always beat you at school.'

I said, 'Could you, now! I can't even remember you. Do you want to see if you can beat me now?'

He said, 'Well, why not?'

'Well, you better tell your mate he better stand up as well and that way you'll have a better chance.'

The little kid had gone back behind the bar. So I sparred up now and gave this schoolyard fighter a full fucking left with the flat of my hand. He went shooting straight over the table like a rocket and cracked his head on the floor! As this troublemaker lay on the floor, black blood oozed out of his head: a bad sign!

The two pals of this man went to get hold of his legs to pull him out of the bar and I went to the toilet. The two conscious ones must have thought I'd left or something, and one of them came back in and put his hand up. He didn't know I was in the vicinity so he didn't know I was behind him coming back in. I said, 'Hey!' I gave him a quick smack on the chin; he was out on the fucking floor like his pal, out like a light.

When the ambulance came for the one I'd flattened in the bar, it was funny because they put an ashtray under his head, and what I was afraid of was the black blood oozing out of his head because it was really thick gooey stuff. I thought, Oh fuck! As he went down he had caught his head.

The ambulance came and took him, but the funny thing was that there was this little fellow who used to do things for the committee and he said to the ambulance crew, 'Don't go yet, there's another fucker out there.' So they had to bring another stretcher for the other fucker as well. The two bloodied men recovered, but I was a bit afraid. As usual, it was all over nothing.

Violence can start over nothing and can happen in a

flash. This was the case when I was in this pub in Merthyr, and there was this fellow, an old fellow; he was very polite and he looked a bit la-de-dah. I didn't think he had it in him. The first person he was arguing with was his friend, and he just leaned on the bar. He was a big fucker, but I didn't think anything about it and normally I don't take my eyes off them ... I thought, He's too fucking old.

He caught me neat, right on the fucking face, and I took one step back and thought, You're not getting away with that, you bastard! I was punching the piss out of him. He kept going down, but I didn't kick him – he'd had enough. I didn't put the boot in to a man older than myself. But this confrontation was out of the blue, out of the fucking blue. That's what I had to face.

After all this had finished, I thought, There's nobody else in this town that will have a go at me, surely to fuck? There's always fresh people coming into the town, passing through for past times and things like that, and another troop would soon come into town.

A lot of the stories I've related to you in this chapter are ones of a local nature. So, when you go out of your own territory, you don't really think that your name will go before you. But there I was, sitting in a pub in Kendal, when a fellow came into the town. I was just starting to enjoy a pint and this fellow comes up, and I've never seen this fucker in my life before. You know what he did – I couldn't fucking believe it – he said, 'I'll fight any fucker in the pub!' I thought, fuck, there's no ending to this violence! But the last words he said after that were, 'Bar fucking Price.'

I've never seen him before. He saw me and said, 'Except

Price. I'll fight any fucker in the town bar Price,' and he was a big fucker. He was having the crack!

An incident that shows how innocent fun can turn nasty happened in the Dowlais Labour Club. I was sitting there having my pint when someone had me around the neck in a headlock and said, 'Drink it up.' He had hold of me and I didn't know who it was. I'd had a fair bit to drink, and didn't recognise him as one of the committee men fooling around with me.

I got up and I launched him over the table and he kept on fucking bouncing like a part-inflated balloon. He ran into the office, so I hit the door and said, 'Come out.' I was hitting the solid wood door so hard that I dented it. I kept hold and held the door shut and eventually the police came in. It was all a misunderstanding, so I got off with just having to pay for a new door; it was an expensive day on the drink and all caused by innocent horseplay.

Everyone in the valleys knew me and, because of that, so many people used my name in the valleys that there must have been at least a hundred times a night that the name 'Malcolm Price' was used.

'I'm a friend of big Malcolm so leave me alone.'

'Touch me and I'll get my best mate Malcolm Price to beat you up.'

'I'm a friend of Price.'

I never knew any of these people who were using my name but, if I had a fiver for every time my name was used for protective purposes by these people to ward off trouble, then I'd be a millionaire many times over by now.

Although many used my name, not many were mistaken

for me. One man, though, who was mistaken for me a few times was Mickey Mochan. He's a big lad and broad with it as well and he said to me, 'I was over the Rhonda the other day and this man said to me, "You're Pricey, aren't you?" And just for the hell of it I didn't say I wasn't you. I've just had a few pints out of it myself.'

I was laughing and said, 'You bastard.'

Another time, I was with Mickey Mochan and he said, 'Call down, Price, on a Saturday because the missus won't let me out.'

So I called down, as we had arranged, and he had the car. It was all right but it was all rusted up, a Morris Oxford it was! It was planned that I would look at the car with a view to buying it, which was his excuse so he could escape out of the house.

So I said to Mochan, 'Look, I might be interested in buying that car.'

He said to his wife, 'I'm going to show Price what engine's in this car. So I'll not be long.'

So off we go in the car and I said, 'It's not a bad engine in this.'

'I'll take you for a ride, I'll take you over to Glyn-Neath,' he said.

'All right, let's go,' I said.

We were going down there and he was doing about 70 – 80mph. It wasn't a bad engine, but the thing was a rust bucket. I was sitting in the front seat and I looked up as something caught my eye.

I could see something tumbling about on the road behind us. I said, 'What was that?'

Something blew off the trees and he said, 'It might be an old cardboard box.'

I said, 'But something has just flew past us … it was a wing, wasn't it? I think you'd better turn off the main road now and get on to the side road if we're going to have a pint, because if you're going to go to Glyn-Neath there is no wing on that … you know, she's just bare.'

I wasn't going to buy the car; it was just an opportunity for him to get out for a few pints because he gets trouble from his wife. We arrived at this place, I forget the name; it was off the main road and we had gone in there now. It had changed hands since we were last in the place. They were now doing meals and things, Saturday lunchtime meals; there was a bit of a restaurant in the back or you could get a bar meal.

There was a couple of old guys, a couple of youngsters and nothing to shout about, and there were people eating meals there, restaurant meals not bar meals.

Mickey Mochan said, 'Nice food, Price.'

I said, 'Lovely, Mick. Very nice. Do you want some food?'

'Aye. Mmm! Are you having some food?' he said.

I knew what he was after when he saw the food. I said, 'No, I'm all right today.'

He went to the toilet to take a leak and I quickly ordered him a meal as a surprise. Ham, egg and chips or something like that. He came back in and he didn't know I had ordered him a meal. I knew he was hungry because he had said, 'I'll have one if you have one.'

I'd paid for the meal, and when the lady who was serving came back she put the meal on the bar.

I said, 'That's yours, get it down you.'

'Oh, no, no! I won't eat it, Price,' said Mick.

I said, 'Well, I won't eat it. It's too late now, it's paid for, so bloody eat it!'

He caused so much of a commotion that the woman looked at the two of us; you could see her looking.

I said, 'I've paid for it, now just eat it! If you don't want it, give it to the old gent there because it's nice and warm.'

The old fellow was glad of it and said, 'Yes, please.'

I said, 'Sound.'

In the meantime, the lady from behind the bar had gone out and must have phoned for the police, as she must have thought there was going to be a bit of trouble. Up came the police from Glyn-Neath, a sergeant and a constable. The rustbucket of a car with its wing missing was right outside, facing the 'In' door of the fucking pub!

Mick said, 'There's police outside and I can see them outside looking at the car.'

I looked up in the air and said, 'Hello, hello, hello! They're outside looking at the car and they'll see there's no bastard wing on it!'

He said, 'What are we going to do now?'

'I don't know what we're going to do; we're in here and the car's out there,' I said.

In they came and they came straight for us, as she must have identified us to the police.

One of the policemen said, 'Where are you two from?'

Now Mochan's the same build as me: like me but bigger; he's also blond but not quite as blond as me. I said, 'From

Merthyr.' I jumped in and answered first because Mick has a stammer.

The sergeant said, 'The two of you?'

'Yes,' I replied.

Mochan tried to say 'yes', but he couldn't get it out fast enough because of his speech problem. 'Name?' he said, and the sergeant pointed to Mickey, but he couldn't get the words out; so I said, 'That's Malcolm Price and I'm Mickey Mochan.'

The policeman stood back and he said, 'Which one of you is fucking Malcolm Price?'

I said, 'I'm Mochan and he's Price.'

Mickey now was stammering so bad he couldn't get it out, 'Eh, eh, eh, eh, eh.' He was like that, see, and I was laughing my fucking head off.

The policeman said, 'Don't fuck me about, which one of you is Price?'

I said, 'Him, that's Price and I'm Mickey Mochan.'

So then he came out with it and I burst out laughing so I had to give in. I said, 'I'm Price.'

'And I'm Mochan. I've been trying to get it out,' said Mick.

The policeman said, 'Fuck, we don't want you over here. Go back to your own side of the fucking mountain.'

I said, 'Yes.'

'And whose fucking car is that?' asked the policeman.

Mochan said, 'We had a- a- a- a- an accident on the way here and a wing was blown off.'

The policeman said, 'Just take the car and fuck off, we'll be glad to see you gone out of this area.'

Top left: Me and my grandmother.

Top right: With Uncle Viv – he was a great fellow.

Bottom left: (From left to right) my mother, me, Aunty Ann and my grandmother.

Bottom right: Me and my sister, with our pet dog Kym in Swansea.

Top: Although my dad wanted me in the ring, I preferred singing in St David's Choir. I'm in the back row, third from the left.

Bottom left: A proud day – I was Barry Peel's best man in Kendal, Cumbria.

Bottom right: The lads on a night out. From left to right: Gwlgm Lewis, Danny Sullivan, me and Mike Mahoney.

Top: With my dear late mum.

Bottom: Days when the hair was bigger! *From left to right*, the late Tommy Bevan, me and Malcolm Pierce.

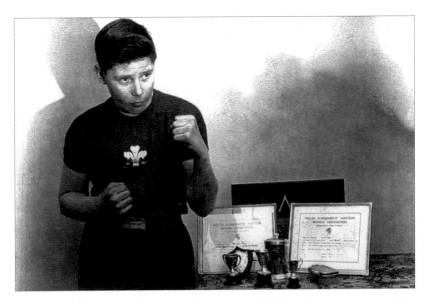

Top: Schoolboy champion. I was always proud to sport the three feathers.

Bottom: The boxing boys. (*Back row, l to r*) Eddie Thomas, Bill Long, Dow James, Hughie Thomas, Mr Bowen and Mr Grant. (*Middle row, l to r*) John Gamble, unknown and me. (*Front row, l to r*) Gerald Jones, Chris Collins and Kevin Flynn.

SPORTRAIT

No. 8 — MALCOLM PRICE

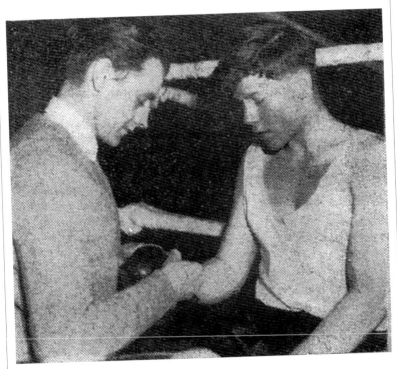

★ By CANDAC

IT comes eo something when a boxer can't get anyone to fight him. But that is the position in which nifty MALCOLM PRICE finds himself.

Although he is only 15 years of age, Malcolm, who lives in Oak-road, Gurnos, Merthyr, scales 10ct. 9lbs.

Malcolm began boxing about four years ago with the Merthyr Boxing Club. He transferred his affections two years ago to Dowlais Boxing Club and has since lost only one of his 16 fights.

In 1955 Malcolm, who was at Queen's-road Secondary Modern School, was a Welsh schoolboy finalist at Coney Beach, Porthcawl, but was beaten.

Last year he became a schoolboy champion. And it is since then that he has been having trouble in getting fights.

There are very few schoolboy boxers of his weight and calibre. And this year he had a walkover in the championship—thus retaining his title.

Malcolm now works in the stores at Thorne Electrical Industries, Merthyr.

TRAINS HARD

On my visit to Eddie Thomas's gymnasium in Penydarren, I have noticed particularly Malcolm's eagerness to train. He is not disgruntled by the fact that his bouts are few and far between. He just keeps himself fit in the knowledge that in the not too distant future he will be good enough to meet older boys of his weight.

Eddie Thomas is convinced that in Malcolm he has an up-and-coming heavy-weight champion.

"He is solid and packs a stinging right hand wallop," says Eddie. "He moves fast and is as fit as a fiddle."

Our picture shows Malcolm having his gloves adjusted at the gym. by Club Treasurer Danny Reardon.

My fists were always attracting attention. Gloving me up for sparring is the late Danny Reardon.

Top: Me with Barry and Brenda Peel on their wedding day. The late Billy Lang is pictured on the far right.

Bottom: Colin Northey's wedding – a happy occasion.

Top: Using my hands for something different! Making music with the boys.

Bottom left: Me with a good old workmate of mine, Lal Lewis, and his sister, Ella, on his 80th birthday.

Bottom right: Me (*centre*) with Ross Crawford (*left*) and another colleague down in Devon.

Top: Little Dai with his motor scraper. Bogged down with friends Russ and me on an open cast coal site in Wales.

Bottom left: Having a pint with Brian Moorhan and Gino Gerbin.

Bottom right: With my good friend Mike Mahoney.

I said, 'But if we touch this car now, we've had two pints, maybe three pints, you'll book us for drink driving as well, or you might have our police over the other side waiting for us at the other end of the road.'

He said, 'No I won't, on my mother's life.'

'Did you hear that,' I said. 'Mochan, the sergeant's mother's life, he won't have police waiting there for us.' So we jumped in the car and fucked off, yeah.

If that wasn't mad enough, one of the maddest fights I ever got involved in happened down in Nelson, down the valley. We were in a nightclub called the Queen of Hearts. There was Mike Mahoney, two other boys and me. I went up to the bar to get my round in and, in the process of putting my drinks on the tray, a fellow tried to push me out of the way. 'Get out of my way, Blondie,' he said.

I looked into his eyes and said, 'Who the fuck are you fucking talking to?'

So I took the drinks back to the boys at the table. I goes back and sees the fellow and he speaks my language when he says, 'Outside, Blondie, we'll sort it out!'

So we get outside and I said, 'There's an alleyway down by there, we'll go down by there.'

As we were walking down, a police car was parked right opposite the club door and two policemen were keeping an eye on the place. I knew there was an alley just down from the club. Out of the blue, this fellow gave me the finest backhander I've ever had, right in front of the police! So I feigned laughing and brushed it off and quietly said, 'It's down by here, you bastard, there's a police car there, you dumb cunt!'

As we were walking down to get to this alleyway, I could hear footsteps coming up behind me. So I had a quick shuffty to see who it was and it was his mate following behind him. Coming up behind the two of them was Mike Mahoney.

So I said, 'Right, up this alley, just a few feet more, off the main road.' I pummelled him with my two hands and he was out like a light! So he's on the ground by the entranceway to the alley. Mahoney head butted the pal of the man I had just sparked out and his went down like the big bag of shit he was.

I thought that was the end of it and prepared to follow up on them with some foot leather, but another pal of the two crocked men came around the corner! So I said, 'Come up here if you want a go!' Two more turned up, so we laced into the three of them and pummelled them down to the ground.

Thinking that was the end of them, I said to Mahoney, 'We'll go back to the club now.' Just as we were making our way out of the alleyway, fucking hell! There was an obstruction, about 20 or 30 of the bastards of all shapes and sizes were coming at us!

I said to Mahoney, 'Fucking hell, where are they all coming from? If any more come then it will be like Custer's last stand, here!'

Mahoney and I levelled the place and there were bodies lying everywhere on the floor. We could only swing our arms so many times before we were elbow deep in blood and gore. I swear, I saw someone poke their finger deep into the eye of one of the mob and, after pulling his finger out, he licked it and spat at the bastards. I said to Mahoney, 'Let's fucking go for it, fuck, 'em!'

I started punching anyone and everyone and every time I hit someone they went down and I kept moving on to the next one. Anyone who's standing in front of me is being knocked out; men were falling all around me and, just as it seemed like it wasn't going to stop, Alsatians were attacking this crowd; the police had arrived!

This mob had now started to pull themselves together and they were pushing the police about and there were more police cars coming all the time. The police were grabbing hold of them and they were pushing the police out of the way. While this was going on, Mahoney and me took the opportunity to edge out of the alleyway.

We were out of the alleyway now and there were even more police and the dogs were going mental and everything. We were in for it. They'd throw the book at us, and we hadn't even started it!

Out of nowhere, a miracle happened! A Merthyr taxi was passing by and the driver recognised us and the driver shouted, 'Pricey! Mahoney!'

We made a bolt for the taxi. 'You dull bastard, open the doors and get us out away from here,' I said to the driver.

The police had the place cordoned off, but we were ducked down in the back of the taxi and it was allowed straight through the police cordon.

We fucked off home! It turned out that this mob was only a whole coachload of rugby players out on the drink! There was just one cheeky bastard in the club that night and it started World War Three. There was a bloodbath down there; they all got locked up, and the police dogs didn't need feeding for a week after that.

This next particular incident happened on a Monday, as there was no work on this specific day. I'd been drinking all day with Mahoney and Mel Shepherd; we were walking up the back way of the town to the Express pub, and it was about six in the evening.

An hour before this, I'd just had an argument with this big lump of a fellow and, as I walked the shortcut, I spotted him, this good for nothing.

My old man had had an argument with this fellow (who I will not name due to the embarrassment it might cause him) at work. I went there and battered him and now was my chance to catch him, as he'd got away earlier on when the police stopped it. This fellow thought he was a bit of a tasty handful, but he had no chance against me.

I said, 'Come here, cunt!'

The fellow runs off and I was fast on his heels; we were evenly matched in the running stakes.

The bastard ran straight into the police station in the belief that I would leave off, but the red mist had overtaken me! As the fellow was making a complaint to the desk sergeant, I ran in and battered him and knocked him clean out. My head was gone and I didn't give a monkey about the consequences. I think I got six months for that one.

I couldn't avoid being charged with that one, but at times, when I was out fighting, the police would just turn a blind eye because they knew I never took liberties with people. The police those days weren't much older then me;

they'd see me perform and then afterwards would usually say, 'Malcolm, that's it now, get home.'

Here's a little anecdote about me, and it's true. I went in to the Great Western pub and went to go into the lounge. The landlord, Alan, said, 'Pricey, you can't go in the lounge – out of there, you and Di Davies.'

I said, 'I spend about £150 a week in this place!'

Alan replied, 'And I turn away about £300 a week away from here; people are frightened to drink with you! You're not doing me any favours!'

CHAPTER 5

THE QUICK BROWN FOX

I was in the alleyway, and it had just started. There was a side door to the next pub down, the Vulcan, and he was coming out of the side door, exiting into the alleyway. There was one down on the floor without a tool and I said, 'Come on, you pair of jumped-up bastards.' The next thing, I was hoisted up in the air and my feet were off the floor. They just waltzed me round the corner, grabbed me under the arms and put my feet back on the floor.

They said, 'You're going home, Price. You've had enough.'

I said, 'I haven't got much to say,' and they took me up home.

I was living in Pontmorlais then and the police said, 'Get him in now – the next time we'll book him.'

I said, 'That's fair enough,' and that was that. That was a fair chance and it was decent treatment. I never really gave any trouble – not unless they deserved it!

I was in the Western pub one night, in the middle of town; Mr and Mrs Brown were the publicans, another well-respected couple. There was this fellow in there and he was trying to get off with the wife of an older friend of mine. This man kept on and on at her, asking her to go to this dance, and, well, of course, her husband wasn't around to defend her from such trash.

There was a dance some-bloody-where. We didn't know this fellow; he wasn't a regular at the pub. I don't know if he was from Merthyr or not, but he was going to some dance or other. His shoes were well polished and everything.

I said, 'You want to leave that lady alone, you know, that's my friend's wife.'

So I said to one of the boys –I think it was Roy Evans but I'm not sure – I said, 'He's a cheeky bastard, he's on to her … cheeky bastard.'

Anyway, he comes up to the bar where it was only Mrs Brown serving, as her old man was upstairs. Now Mrs Brown was so short that she couldn't see over the bar counter. She was looking up at us from behind the bar, but the bar was up past our waists.

I said to Roy, 'He's still on with her!'

I got a tap on the shoulder; she'd come up to me and said, 'Pricey, I can't stick with it no more.'

I said, 'Sit back down, it will only take two seconds, sit down.'

The woman was agitated; she'd had enough of being accosted by this out-of-town stranger. So I caught Mrs

Brown on the arm and said, 'Give her a half, I'll pay for this.'

The friend's wife said, 'I don't want this.'

I said, 'Sit down, now, it's all taken care of.'

She replied, 'Thank you, Price.'

I said, 'Sound.'

Then her friends, two older ladies, came into the pub. This fellow came up to the bar and Mr Brown, who had just come down, served this fellow with another pint and back he goes with his drink. He was heading way back in the direction of my friend's wife so, when he put the pint down, I flings him around and bumps him out; out like a light!

'Oh, thank you, Price,' my friend's wife said in respect of what I'd just done. She went on to say, 'You just took a load off my chest.'

In order for Mrs Brown not to see what had gone on, I had to make a quick decision! Remember, she couldn't see over the bar. This fellow was now on the floor doing an impression of a rug, funnily enough, by the fire. I dragged him up to the bar and left him lying right up at the edge of bar where it met the floor by the foot rail. We took his shoes off and I put them on the fire.

Mrs Brown came back in and she said, 'What's that I can smell in here?'

I said, 'I don't know, Mrs Brown.'

'What's burning on the fire?' she said as she came out with the poker, but she saw the body beneath the bar counter. I had already pissed off and gone to hide in the toilets. Eventually, when I came out of the toilet she says, 'What happened to that lad?'

I said, 'He just seemed to collapse and I was going to tell you, he just collapsed in a heap. He must be drunk.'

So anyway, she'd had enough of him and she said, 'Oh yes, Mr Brown was on to me about him; I'll have to phone the ambulance.'

'No!' they said, so we put some water on his face, got him up and walked him to the door and escorted him out of the pub, shoeless, and that was the end of that.

Mrs Brown had been watching him and said, 'It's getting like the Wild West around here.' Well, it was the Western pub!

Mrs Brown said to me, 'Are you sure you weren't involved in this, Price?'

I said, 'No, Mrs Brown, he was drunk and he was after Mrs what's-her-name for that.'

Mrs Brown laid down the law when she said, 'We don't want any trouble and we are not going to have any trouble!'

We were, all of us, Mike, Harry and me, like that: 'Yes, Mrs Brown,' and 'No, Mrs Brown,' but they served us and it was all forgotten. That's how it was, great big hard men taking a dressing down from a woman who wasn't even tall enough to see over a bar top!

Knocking out such a man and doing what I did was nothing unusual to me, but in a well-to-do pub, even in Merthyr, they wouldn't stand for it.

Although I was involved in many more minor skirmishes, they aren't worth mentioning. I still had the calling of the wild – animals and birds brought out the best in me. When I was living in a flat opposite the Prince Charles Hospital, just by the side of the Matchstick Man, big Edward Worrel was going to get me a fox.

He asked, 'You want a fox cub, do you?'

I said, 'Aye, try and make it a slate-blue coloured one.'

The slate-blue colour, a bluey-grey, shows that the animal is young enough to be tamed to bring them up and have them as tame pets. I didn't want any other colour because then they are too old to accept you; they bite! I had this thing about foxes and a fellow I knew had one for a pet.

So I said to Edward, 'Get me a cub.'

He said, 'Right.'

I enquired, 'When will it be?'

'We're going out lamping on Saturday night, and we might come across one.'

He was going out with a lamp or some bloody thing; he always used to go lamping with his dogs; he had good dogs. Anyway, out he came to the Iron Horse where we kept a useful old box. The landlord of the pub was called Alan but we used to call him Old Shagger. He was an old fighter and his pub was the kind of pub you used to go in and if you had nowt, you would shout up the stairs to Sally and get a drink until you next got paid.

I said to all with me, 'Is there any chance of a sub?'

'Shout up the stairs and ask her 'til payday,' was the reply.

I'd shout up the stairs.

'Tell him to take it out of the till,' came the reply.

I said, 'Only till Thursday, 'til payday.'

'Righto,' she said; that was sound.

In comes Edward Worral with the fox. He put the sack alongside me, and he said, 'Don't open it now or it will be running everywhere.'

I said, 'Righto.'

I was so excited that I said I'd take her home myself, and go a bit early. I only supped half of my drink and off I went in anticipation of taming my slate-coloured fox. I took her home and locked myself in the cupboard with this fox so as to prevent her from escaping.

I gently opened the sack, slowly eased open the top of the sack and there she was … red, wasn't she! She was awfully light in weight; there was no weight to her at all. I remember Edward saying, 'She hasn't had no food, no milk or nothing at all.'

A few times, I was trying to coax her out of the sack; but she was red and three-quarters grown. That night, I stayed on the floor with her and I kept coaxing her and talking to her in the same soft voice. I didn't raise the tone of my voice, and I could see that she was beginning to become comfortable with my presence.

I was lying down on the cold hard floor; there was only the electric meter, the fox and I in this cupboard. As the first shafts of daylight approached, she was sitting there in all her glory and after a while she would try and get her body round the meter; she was trying to run behind the meter all the time.

As the daylight came up through the cupboard window, my outstretched and aching hand holding the food was in the same position as it had been some many hours earlier. The red fox, she looked at me! She timidly came towards me and, whilst averting eye contact, she held my arm with one of her paws and gently took the food from my hand with her mouth.

After taking the food, she tried to get behind the meter.

She had taken the food from my hand, and that was half the battle. But I still had to keep my voice in the same pattern or it would have caused her confusion and I would have had to start all over again to gain her trust.

I had made my decision: I was going to keep the fox. I had done the hardest work. She was only a year as she was, but she had a terrible smell. The thing is, I just wanted to keep the fox, but I thought to myself, should I or shouldn't I?

Maybe I caught a glimpse of myself mirrored in the way the fox wanted to come forward to take the friendship offered; regardless of how hard it tried to overcome its natural instinct, it was always wary of being struck with unmeasured violence!

Maybe if I had been caught young and had been held warmly with a set of strong arms when in need of such love from my father, then maybe I would have been a different person. Was I trying to exorcise the demons of my past by showing a wild animal some love and compassion? Who knows!

Eventually, Freddy Bramley begged me and begged me for the cub for himself. Freddy Bramley and me knew each other from being kids, from birds' nests days and everything. He was a good artist, a marvellous artist. He begged the cub off me for his son, so in the end I gave him the cub for his son.

The fox, she was kept in a box outside and eventually she escaped to freedom. Was that what happened to me? Had I been put in that boxing ring for the pleasure of others, yet left to conjure up my own ways of passing time, just as the fox had been left to do in that box? Anyway, that was the red fox!

Bramley, poor bugger, was a talented boy. He could just look at a tree and carve out walking sticks. He was a lad as well, another character. A right character, but he was a good mate as well. We did all sorts; we went in search of birds' nests together as youngsters, from an early age. Bramley, he died young, it was cancer.

I don't know what it is, but I know a lot of hard men who just go daft when they see a lovely fluffy animal. Like Mal Powell who committed suicide, he was always sad but thought the world of his dog, he did. He was the original Hatchet Man. He didn't give them any warning when he hit them, he just clonked them over the head with a hatchet. He was a big lad, but he was a quiet lad and he always used to talk about animals and all that … but his dog, if he had some meat he would supply the dog first.

He chucked himself off Cefn Bridge. Even though he was a nice fellow, I lost my head with him once. The Locomotive pub or something like that it was and he was in the bar; it was a club then. He didn't have the dog with him that day.

He was there and he said, 'I think you're wrong there.' It was over nothing really.

I said, 'Hey, hey, hey, who do you think you're talking to then?'

Big Mal, he was a big bastard: he was taller than me and a lot bigger as well: if you got him in a good mood he was a nice person. When he lost his head, though, he was a loser; he was that type of fellow.

Anyway, I lost it with him and he could see from the look in my eyes that he was in for it, so he ran out of the pub with me in hot pursuit!

In those days, the police had mini cars. Big Mal could run, but I wasn't a very fast runner. I wasn't built for that, but neither was he come to think of it, but he could fucking move. I chased after the big bastard, but he was too quick for me, but I wasn't giving up that easy!

The chase was on, and after a while I was out of breath and gasping for air. I stopped outside St David's Church. I was shouting, 'Stand still, you bastard! You big bastard!' By this time, he was up at the castle and he too was having a blow and I was having a blow. And then I would start to run at him and he'd be off. We were going hell for leather up the main street and everyone was looking.

We had only just stopped when he shouted down to me, 'Come on, come on then!' So he was just going to go when this police car, a little mini, pulled up.

The policeman in the car said, 'What's the matter, Price, what's the trouble?' He tried to grab my arm.

I gasped, 'Give me a fucking lift; I want to try and catch him up.'

With that, the policeman pushed me away and took off like a rocket. I was going to use the mini car to catch up with that big bastard; it was all a laugh and the police never bothered. He's a big miss is big Mal Powell, God rest his soul.

Although I was always having fights and troubles with people, this particular day it was my love of animals that got me locked up when I was living in some flat. A neighbour kept some lovely pedigree Alsatian dogs tied up in a hut. The dogs were howling out their frustrations and whimpering out their pain of being restrained to no ends. They never got let out or taken for exercise.

I too needed a little exercise, as I had piled on the pounds. Every time I walked past the gate, I used to run to the end. I had to lose weight because I was close on seventeen-and-a-half stone. I started putting on these plastic bags and all my tee shirts over the top of them, and a big coat. I looked like the Michelin Man!

I started walking this dog I had borrowed, and she was a big bitch, as big as any dog and she was overweight as much as I was overweight, so I lost about five, five-and-a-half stone and the dog slimmed down quite nicely too.

Yes, I lost about five-and-a-half stone by cutting down on food, cutting down on all the fat, no bread, no chips, no nothing in the frying pan at all, and I did it. The hospital had to put me through this scanning machine for a back problem I had. The problem is that if you're over 17 stone they won't put you through the MRI scanner because of the power of the machinery and the cost if it breaks.

I thought, Why should I walk someone else's dog when I can have a dog of my own? At this time I was living in a dingy flat and these neighbours were just letting these Alsatians go to waste. I didn't want to interfere, but my love of animals was compelling me to do something about it and the more the animals howled the more agitated I became at the pain they were obviously suffering due to being confined for 24 hours of the day.

I thought, If that's the way you like to live, you choose

the way you live, don't you, but there's no need to make animals suffer because of it.

It was the incessant howling noise that I couldn't put up with that went on 'til four o'clock in the morning. I was working on earthmoving machinery and had to be up at 6am. Some days, I wouldn't need to get up, as the machine might not be needed, but I still couldn't sleep for the noise, and it was starting to wear my patience down.

Regardless of not getting a lie-in, I felt sorry for these Alsatians. One day, my front door was open, I was sat on the bed and my mate was in the armchair. It was a lovely sunny summer's day. I said, 'Those dogs are whining, locked up in there.' There were some turkey bits from the market, which I used to slip in to the Alsatians, because the owner didn't feed them at all. It was the son that had the dogs and she used to say that he was never there.

I used to offer to take the dogs out, 'I'll walk the dogs for you.'

She said, 'My son wouldn't be beholden to you.'

I said, 'You can't leave dogs locked up in the shed, it's cruel.' I went on to say, 'If you don't open the shed it will get to them.'

And old Pauline – a neighbour who's passed away now, said, 'It's disgusting!'

All the neighbours, when they were talking, they wouldn't bother them.

One Saturday night, I came home by taxi. The taxi driver, Ian Baldy; he likes animals and he'd seen the poor Alsatians many times.

I said, 'Put me out at the gate, Baldy.'

Ian replied, 'Oh no! No, no!'

He knew what I was like! I could put my fingers through the gaps in the wood of the hut; I could stroke them with my fingers.

'Pricey,' he said '… have you?' He knew what my game was. I replied, 'Aye.'

The dogs were out of the hut and at last they had some respite, even if it was short lived.

I got up one day, and the son who was supposed to look after the dogs was out. I didn't look at him; I had the back door open facing him. These two big Alsatians had charged in through my open door and were bowling me over; they went straight into the kitchen to see what I had for them. They knew me straight away. They ended up with some nice bits of turkey.

Then one night … how the hell did he get in, like? I put the light on and the police had to come and fetch him in the morning. I took the dog, the oldest dog, and it was as if he was at home. A lovely dog but if anyone came near him he'd snap at them!

Then she must have called the police the day that I had a machete. I was going to tell her that if she didn't let the dogs out then I was going to chop the gate down with the machete. With that she said, 'You've got a big knife there!' My intention was to chop the gate down and let the dogs out. I had to go round the other side then and I was telling her, 'If you don't come out from that shed I'm going to chop the gate down.'

She wouldn't open the door, so the next thing there were flashing lights and two police cars and I got a good searching as well. They saw the machete and said, 'Price, give me the knife.'

They took the machete off my belt and I said, 'You're locking up the wrong bastard, it was them bastards.' I was trying to tell them all this: I should have done it when I was sober and showed them what was what, but in the end the court made a big case of this but she never turned up, the bastard.

Yes, I was locked up with Alsatians! I was only charged with threatening behaviour or something and it was only a short visit to the local court.

I know what members of Greenpeace must feel like when they save some sort of animal. Mind you, I don't agree with these animal liberation people putting bombs in letters. If you can't do it yourself by your own action then you shouldn't do it.

I won the day! I had the Alsatians taken off them; one was distributed out to Carmarthen way and the youngest dog, the pup, was somewhere else; so they had a home to go to. I was glad and old Pauline was over the moon and it was worth it.

People knew I loved animals, but one day someone said I was a bighead to Edward Worral. So Edward played a practical joke on me that backfired on him. He's a big lad, one of the best, and he's a real cracker with horses. We were in the pub, Donald McCarthy and me; Donald knew the crack because he's done a lot of time. I was drinking and I counted that I'd had four pints and I'd had enough. Anyway it was a Saturday.

Big Ed came to me and said, 'Price, are you going home?

Do you want a lift?'

I said, 'Ah, great. Save me catching a taxi.'

He said, 'You going now? Well, I'll see you outside in about five minutes.'

We went on the balcony outside; I would have to cancel the taxi I'd ordered. I didn't know what car Worral had. All I could hear was clip-clop, clip-clop and it was he, big Edward Worral, on this fucking big horse! I thought, fuck me, I can't ride one of them! He wanted me to get on the horse with him. He was a big fucking stallion, this horse!

'Fucking hell!' I said. 'I can't ride, I've never rode and I've never done a lot with horses.'

He said, 'Jump up.'

I said, 'Reverse ...'

So they had to come out of the pub and bunk me up on to the horse, which the willing crowd did.

He said, 'Do you want me to hold on to you? Just put your arms around me and hold on tight.'

I said, 'Sound.'

We were doing fine and he was driving the horse and I was behind him holding my hands tight around him. We were on Brecon Road, in Merthyr, just past the side of the park, just past the main gates and a car pulls up! All the boys from the pub see me and out from the window came a fucking big stick and someone hit the horse on the arse!

I was trying to kick the guy with the stick away with my foot, but I hit the horse and he galloped off like Red Rum!

'Hold on! Hold on ... leave go, leave go! Price, you're killing me, I can't breathe.' The faster the horse was galloping, the tighter I was holding on. I was squeezing all of the air out of Worral's lungs. This is when it backfired on Worral; I'm surprised I didn't squeeze his liver out of his arse, as I had a tight hold on him.

So I said, 'Take it off the road, get up through the park; they can't follow us through the woods.'

That's the way we went, up through the park, and the horse was panicking as well. We gets right up to the roundabout, through the hedge and, as we were coming up on to the road, the horse did a little wiggle, and he was a big horse, a fucking big horse. I was broadside and Edward said, 'Hold on!' And, within a split second of Edward saying that, we both fell off the horse.

Across the road, a few yards away, was a policeman booking someone. He had his car boot open and they found suspicious goods in it. All I could see was a pair of boots in front of me, black boots. Edward had hurt his ribs, probably by my squeezing him, and I had hurt my bastard arm and so I said, 'Hello, hello, hello!'

The policeman said, 'What's happening here? We've got Price the jockey and who is it, Edward Worral?' It wasn't half a laugh, and he soon left us and the horse alone in the confusion.

CHAPTER 6

UNEXPECTED GUEST

Confrontations come in many guises, but the usual type was that of a young buck wanting to prove himself. There was one particular fellow, a big lad who was younger than me, and I think he worked out on the weights a bit. He always wanted to beat me at arm-wrestling so as to prove something.

When he asked me to arm-wrestle, I said, 'I can't be bothered, I've just come from work.' This challenge went on for about three months and, whenever I went through the bar of the Iron Horse pub, he was always sitting there.

I would go up to the bar and the barman would say, 'I see your mate's in again, Price.'

'I can see him, if he wants me tonight I could give him a good hiding, well perhaps that's what it will take to stop him,' I replied.

I thought, Oh well, I'll have a go at him, so I easily brought his insignificant challenge to an end when I put his arm down, and that was the end of that ... Or so I thought!

'Left hand,' he said, and so I put him down with the other hand as well.

I said, 'That's fair enough now,' and thought it would stop.

The next time he was in, he came up to me again and wanted to have another go and he was playing the same record over again. He was a weird fellow; he used to look straight through you as if you weren't there.

In the end, I had no option but to hit him over the head and put him in the ambulance; he was a bastard anyway. I couldn't stick any more of it. I never saw him again after that.

I was used to that sort of macho man confrontation, but a particular incident I am about to tell you about took me aback. One night, it must have been about two or three o'clock in the morning, I took a member of my family in.

Sometime in the middle of the night, she said, 'There's someone kicking the door in!' Sure enough, that was the case and whoever was doing the kicking was making a determined effort to get in! I thought that if it were one of the boys then he wouldn't be banging on the door like a lunatic.

I went to the door and tentatively opened it. There, standing right in my way was this big monstrous face; it was grisly and I slammed the door shut! That wasn't one of the boys; It's an evil bastard, I thought to myself! I didn't know who it was; I didn't even know the man. He was a big bastard, tall; he was like someone from an asylum. That's who I thought it was, I didn't know him at all.

I thought to myself, the first thing you want to do is put your trousers on. I felt I couldn't fight without my trousers on, so I went back and put them on as fast as I could, and it only took me a minute. I mean, I could just see the newspaper headlines: 'Pricey caught fighting with his trousers off'!

The next thing, I had a big brass key from a twenty-first birthday hanging on the wall and I grabbed hold of that. I had to find out who he was and, in a flash, I was out of the door and down the steps, armed with the key; I was more than ready to fight him. The initial shock of seeing a Frankenstein monster had now turned to rage.

I went and I looked this way and that way and there he was right on the end of the veranda! I had him! He was fucked because he couldn't go any further due to the railings at the end. He was caught in a dead-end and this was a second-floor balcony ... he had no escape route, not unless it was by getting past me!

That was his only way; he would have to come past me now to get back down the steps. I said, 'Who are you, you fucking idiot?' The next thing I knew, he came bowling up to me. I didn't know this fellow and I kept hitting him. I gave him the thrashing of his life and I didn't stop pounding away at him until he went down and then I laced into him with the mandatory follow-up boot.

I said, 'You're going over the fucking top, you are.' I was going to pick him up off the ground and throw him over the balcony, but, by this time, due to all of the commotion and the noise, there were a few people gathered around. And to make matters worse, I could see lights going on in the neighbours' houses across the road, opposite.

People were on the spot and they had this man picked up by now and he was bleeding claret by the bucketload. I was covered in his blood from head to toe. He didn't know me. Soon, the police came up and started asking what had happened.

I said, 'This fellow tried to break into my house; my flat.'

The policeman said to me, 'How is he bleeding this bad, Price?'

There on the ground, where the man was picked up from, was a lake of blood.

I said, 'I don't know. What am I supposed to do, let him just kick my door down. It's a fucking mess! I don't know this fellow, has he escaped from some asylum or something, is that it?'

The policeman said, 'We don't know who he is, Price.'

I replied, 'Well, I don't know who he is either, I just don't know. He just tried to break in to my flat, just get the fellow away from here and be quick about it. What am I supposed to do, leave him in my flat?'

The policeman checked over the man's head and he said, 'Well, I don't know about that.'

'But he tried to get into my door,' I repeated.

He said, 'So that's it, then?'

This man was hospitalised for about a week with serious concussion and he had to use sticks and that to help him get about. I mean, you just don't kick someone's door in and expect to get away with it, although judging by the way the courts sentence people for defending their properties these days it would be easier just leaving your door open with a notice saying 'HELP YOURSELF'.

UNEXPECTED GUEST

After the police had gone, I picked up this thing, this card thing that had come out of the man's pocket; it must have come out as I was jack-hammering him with punches. There wasn't any money in it, but there was this photo and this bus driver's licence. So he was a bus driver; and a lunatic bus driver at that! What the fuck was he doing kicking my door in at two o'clock in the morning? I had to find out.

This driver only lived about two blocks away from me, and I'd never seen the fellow before this happened. After a bit of checking around, I found out his address and I knew what his name was – it was right next to his picture on the card. I enquired about him and, sure enough, he had been in hospital for a week.

I thought, I must return this favour of kicking my door in. I was told he was out of hospital and I prepared myself to go through the motions of payback time! So I knew where he lived now, I had the street name and the door number. I went to the house to return the visit. Now it was my turn to kick his door in!

What I didn't know was that, as I was banging away at his front door, his wife had only just let him out through the back door and he was jumping over neighbours' gardens like a mad March hare to get away from me. Funny how he didn't need a walking stick to help him.

His wife came to the door and I said, 'Where is he, where's he at?' I pushed past the side of her, ran up the stairs and I looked in all of the bedrooms, under the beds and in the wardrobes – nothing!

'He's not in, Malcolm, he's not in, Malcolm,' his missus kept telling me.

Someone must have phoned for the police by now and, funnily enough, she sat down with me and pleaded, 'Please sit down and let me have ten minutes of your time. He didn't know what he was doing that night. I was just going to take him to hospital and he's gone running through all the gardens and everything, he's not here, see.'

She had let him out of the back door. I could see him in my mind – he would have been off like a greyhound being released from the traps. I just went for the door like a bull at the gate. I'd be behind bars now because I'd have killed him, as I had that in mind. By the time she had calmed me down, the police were at the door.

I said, 'I don't even know him.'

She said, 'Neither does he know you. I think somebody had put him up to this.'

I asked, 'Why my door?'

She tried to explain his actions. 'Well, someone must have told him where you live and put him up to it. He's never been like this in his whole life. Someone must have spiked his drink with drugs or whatever. It's not in his nature.' It was then that I felt sorry for her.

Then the police came to the door and they asked, 'Have you had a break-in?'

She nodded in my direction and said, 'He knocked hard and I let him in. There's been no break-in here.' With that explanation, the police left.

I thought, that's fair crack.

She said, 'He's terrified now to go outside the door and leave the home.'

There was no explanation for what he did; somebody

had spiked his drink, that's all she could put it down to. He picked the wrong door, didn't he? Or he picked the right door. Just imagine if he had picked someone's door that couldn't have handled him or herself; it doesn't bear thinking about. You get these random attacks on people by complete strangers just for the sake of it, just to see what it's like to spill someone else's blood.

They get the taste for murder, a bloodlust! I can tell you, the sight of blood is never as pretty as the movies make it out to be. You can be pummelling someone to death, but when you see that dark-coloured blood, well … it's a bad sign! Life imprisonment flashes before your eyes, hope and despair mixed into one feeling. So I'm pleased it was my door he tried to kick in and not some pensioner's door.

That incident just dried up and I left it at that, with the kids at the man's house crying. What makes people flip like that? I couldn't tell you! I just said, 'Why?' I was at home in bed; I wasn't in a dancehall or a pub and out of all the millions of other doors out there, trouble still found its way to my door.

Was it some sort of magnetic attraction I was giving out? I don't know, but the only logical answer was that someone must have put this gormless fool up to this. Even his wife said someone must have put him up to it.

But he was a bus driver, for Christ sake! He was a very big guy and I didn't know his face when he stuck it through the door. I panicked because it wasn't one of the boys. I flipped! The red mist came over me and I went into one!

Well, I'll tell you one thing, I'm lucky the crowd of

people and the police came along or I might have been doing a long stretch. Whilst I had a hold of him I was definitely in the mind to throw him over the balcony; that was my intention and I had him halfway up on to the veranda rails.

One thing that did save him in the long-term was his wife. What he did was somebody else's mad high jinks; he could have signed his own death warrant doing that. But she couldn't explain it and to this day I can't explain why she hasn't been able to do that.

When trouble comes to your door in the middle of the night, it can be confusing, but trouble in pubs and clubs for me was second nature. I remember when I was out for a quiet drink with a man whose mother was a pub landlady. We were in the Growen pub in Dowlais on a Saturday afternoon. Not a pick of trouble crossed my path, until I met with a shambolic crowd of people fighting each other as they came out of the man's mother's pub.

They were still fighting as they were coming out and it was some of the locals, wasn't it? So, as they were coming through the door, we were putting them down like bowling pins. They landed on the floor, star gazing on their backs!

I went for his mother the landlady, but that's over with now. At that time I was having a lot of phone calls, and I didn't give many people my phone number, but they had the pub's number and were constantly phoning me at the pub to catch me in and it was causing some annoyance to me.

I was becoming a popular man and people wanted my services. There was a fellow from Newport who had market stalls; I thought they must have been travellers. This was a stall selling clothes. I was getting lots of such phone calls from people crying out for my help and asking me to do favours for them and all that.

One fellow even wanted me to do his wife in or at least put her in hospital for a long time.

'You better do that job yourself or find someone who can do it for you because I'm not getting involved in that,' I told him. I was starting to get a name, but I didn't need a name for being a woman-killer ... no thanks.

This man with market stalls came up in a car to see me. He wasn't a bum; he lived on one of those new estates outside of Newport, Caerleon. I was told, 'He's coming up to see you this afternoon; he's got his own market stall. This other fellow is trying to pinch his pitch on the markets.' This was a mini turf war over market stalls, that's the way I took it to be.

So this man said to me, 'The car, a big white Mercedes, is coming up now and you can just go down with him in the Mercedes to sort the trouble.'

I said, 'Oh! We have an old van outside, we'll follow him when he arrives.' We had a chat first in his house; I could see that him having the Mercedes and the posh house meant that he had a few bob.

The market man wanted me to frighten off his competitor who was trying to steal his pitch on the gaffs (markets). A plan was arranged to lure his enemy in. My man, who I was now helping out with his problem, had arranged to be in the same pub as the man he wanted me to have words with.

He said, 'I'll wink at you when he comes through the door.'

'All right.' I said and he gave me a description and this and that and I said, 'I'll watch for you winking at me, then.'

So Mickey Mochan and me are having a pint in the bar and my man's pint was on the other table. We were in the place early on. The next thing, the fellow's competitor walks in, my man goes up to the bar and he tips me the wink.

I mouthed the word, 'Right.'

I said to Mickey Mochan, 'When he goes for a leak, I'll go in after him and, if anyone comes in that's with him, you just keep them out of the way 'til I deal with it.'

Eventually, he went to the toilet and I called Mickey in. There was no one else in the toilets except for an old fellow who soon ran out when he saw us.

I said to Mickey, 'Stay here and mind the door.'

The man I wanted a word with was having a piss. I put my hand on his shoulder and I spoke very close to his ear, 'You'd better leave off the pitch you're trying to muscle in on otherwise you'll have to use a straw to piss out of, as you can't piss with a missing dick and you will be put into hospital for a very long fucking time.' He didn't know what to say; he was too taken aback.

Then I said, 'You either get it or you fucking don't and the house goes with it and everything you've got will go with you!'

I never heard anything else after this. The market trader paid me half the money up front before I settled this fellow and the other half afterwards.

People were coming from all over the place for my services. Word was spreading like wildfire over a good few valleys; there was the Rhonda and I don't know how I was getting all these phone calls. Obviously people were passing the number on for me.

I had to be careful in how I went about taking these debt collecting jobs because I didn't know the type of person it was that would be asking me to do things for them. I mean, they could have been setting me up for the police. I was always panicky about the CID division of the police sending in undercover cops, if you know what I mean. I could have gone into business and made a real big-time score, some people do, don't they? I'm not prepared to say too much about that side of things!

Looking back on that side of things, I know people used me for their own advantage; they would entice me in to their circle of friends and then put propositions to me. I was my own boss, accountable to no one! I was the one who made my own decisions, good or bad. I didn't have a team backing me up and I didn't need one, but I always had the support of some true friends if ever I needed it.

One lesson I learned from all of this, and that was a hard one, for all of the good I did people, it was never remembered. I was the one doing jail, not them. Apart from a small circle of close loyal friends, I was and am on my own. People befriended me for what they could get in terms of using me when they had trouble. I've turned my back on that sort of thing now. I've found myself and I like myself, but I don't like unexpected guests kicking my front door in!

CHAPTER 7

ON THE ROAD

I was working down the M4 where they built the first bridge. The great thing about being on the road was I got to meet all the boys working for different plant and earthmoving companies. We were all working together on different machines and everything. Big Lyn Richards, a few of the boys, some of the older men and me were driving the trucks down there and we met these local Welsh boys who were from Caerphilly, Cardiff, and so on. They promised to have a drink with us.

There were one or two machine men with them as well; I had previously worked with them when I was working down in Chudleigh, Devon. I was on the by-pass with these boys and we all knew each other.

I knew everyone except for this big dark mixed-race fellow, who didn't say anything; he was just looking but I didn't pay him any mind. After work, we all had a pint and this dark silent fellow had still said nothing at all. Eventually, his lot said they were thinking of heading back and they wanted to go. Without any warning, he grabbed hold of a lame fellow from Pontypool who was working with us and said, 'Come on!'

I said, 'Don't pull him, man! Look at his leg, mate!'

What he said caught me by surprise: 'Which is Price, are you Price?'

I knew as soon as he mentioned the name, I had this feeling, and he said, 'Outside now, big man,' just like that.

All I said was, 'I don't even know you, to be honest.'

'Well,' he said, 'we'll still go outside.'

I knew then that they had brought him up especially so as to do me over; so little Mel was with me and he said, 'Careful that he's not tooled up, Pricey!'

I said, 'I know the crack.'

He was a rough boy from Caerphilly, this bloke. I said, 'There's a car park there.'

'Yes,' he said. He was all for it and he came up especially to have a go at me. He didn't manage to reach the car park! As I was in the alley I thought, I'll do him here and get it over with.

I said, 'This is far enough, now.'

He turned around quickly, but I was first in with a walloping punch. I've always landed a straight right but people didn't know that I could use my elbows, my knees and every bastard thing else.

Anyway, I caught him and he grabbed hold of me as he went back against the wall and I gave him another one straight out of the Christmas cracker, straight in to the googlies! Now, because he was straight up against the wall, I butted him and he just dropped like a stone.

No doubt about it, he was a strong boy and, as I went to walk away, for good measure, I battered him some more and put the boot in. When he was lying there, stone cold, I pulled his shoes off and threw them over the car park wall. I did that so he would know what it felt like to be lame.

I'd finished him and I was about to walk away for the last time, but he still had life in him and he grabbed hold of my ankle; I finished him off properly then. Someone had obviously paid him to do a job on me.

Oh yes, they had set me up all right; saying, 'Price won't come out of this.' It was clear that they had a bet on the big one.

Little Mel Shepherd said, 'You're in for a terrible shock! Pricey could always hold, like a fucking Nellie.'

Then I walked back through the door and they all looked at me in astonishment, as if what I had just done was unbelievable. I didn't know who this dark fellow was until afterwards and I'd found out that he had put a lot of boys on the floor down there in Cardiff and he was pretty useful. So I said, 'You had better go and pick your mate up.' I could see from the smiles on their faces that it was the boys that we worked with in Newport who were involved in the set-up. But there were some from Cardiff and one or two from Caerphilly, too. They had definitely brought him, but I don't know how much he was being paid. It was a set-up because they'd admitted to Mel that they had brought this fellow up to 'see Price'. The guy was obviously sure of himself. I didn't know this; I thought he was just a quiet man. I knew he wasn't a plant driver or anything like that. Six months later, this dark fellow was up on a manslaughter charge when he killed someone down in Caerphilly – he got ten years.

Earthmoving jobs took me all over the place. One time I was on the Cockermouth by-pass working for Tarmac, and I think we were staying at The Fox and Hounds, in Cockermouth, on the main road. A local fellow was giving good digs to me and a load of Scottish boys who came from Stewart Hewton (or Hewton Stewart) Plant in Scotland.

Up there, I met Ray Blaylock and his friend David and another two machine drivers who had been all over the motorways and everywhere. They were very good friends of mine. It was funny because I walked in one night and there they were.

I got on well with the people! Big Geordie, a good driver, was a good friend. I remember Big Geordie and me going to this do. We were in the pub and we'd been warned by the landlady, 'Boys, I'd love to serve you, you're a good set of boys, but you'll have to cool it for a couple of weeks now. I can tell you where to go, there's this pub opening. Go in to Workington and there is a club opening straight away; as we shut, they open.'

So the Scots boys and me, off down the road we went, with Big Geordie in tow as well. We all went to this club and, sure enough, it was open. Eventually, it was my round. There was about six of us now so I thought, I'll have to get a tray for these to get them back to the table.

I went up to the counter and there was a guy next to me reading the paper. He had his head right into it. I turned with one of the trays and caught him with it. I said, 'I'm sorry.' The man looked over the paper and it was little Joe Walsh, who was working with me for Wimpey when we had previously worked at Cockermouth.

I said, 'What are you doing here, Joe, you old fucker?' He'll be retired now and we still keep in touch. That's how it was, you'd be moving about the jobs so much that you never knew who you'd bump in to ... a small world.

Anyway, Russell and me were down at the Chudleigh by-pass job, in Devon. Chudleigh is only a village with not a lot of nightlife so we used to get in to Torquay and all that on weekends and there were some smart girls there too.

We were in the pub one night in Chudleigh, just having a quiet drink, when the quietness was soon disturbed when these two brothers took a disliking to us. I think they must have been local bastards and they didn't want us there. They used to work for the local quarry and they were a load of shit. One of them lost his head, because we were getting in their hair: they were getting a bit pissed off with us for no other reason than us being there. They didn't want us there, and they thought we should go somewhere else. In the end I said, 'I think the fucking two of you better come outside.'

Russell said, 'I don't want to,' because Russell wasn't a fighting man and he was suffering with his ulcers and stomach and things like that and I didn't want to see him in any trouble. So I said to the two troublemakers, 'You'd better come outside.' I knocked one clean out of the car park and, while I was doing this, the other one tried to get away.

I got hold of him and I was beating the shit out of him. I had him bent over a car bonnet when he said, 'I've had enough, I've had enough!'

I said, 'I'll tell you when you've fucking had enough, you bastard!' So I left the two of them on the ground for the ambulance to clear up and, in the end, Russell and me fucked off to somewhere else.

I wasn't one for drinking on my own, only a sad man can drink on his own. I wanted to enjoy the company of my mates. When I was working on the M56, Mad Mick and me were on the beer; they sent us home on a Sunday because we were pissed out of our skulls.

Mickey was driving a motorised scraper, but the box on the machine that holds up to 50 tons of earth was empty so he easily drove up an embankment. He was now travelling along the top of the soil heap, I wanted to be up there with him, but my machine was carrying a full load. I couldn't make the climb with the machine in this state, so I had to drive further along and reach a road that would take me there. Mickey had run into a fence and all of these cows came charging out and that was game over for us, as the cows wouldn't move!

We were in the pub early that day; it was still daylight and we were steaming drunk! That night, we slept under the caravan, not in it, as we couldn't get in it because the lads wouldn't open the caravan door to us … I wonder why!

When we were working on the M4, there were a lot of

boys there from a lot of motorways; some of them had their own private site lorries there. I remember on this job I wanted to use one of the lorries. A big guy stood up and told me there's no way I'm using his lorry! I hadn't even asked him.

I said, 'Come outside by here.' I knocked his front teeth out for him and we became good friends after that. Oh, and I got to borrow his lorry too!

The next day, the foreman came up to us and said, 'It's up to you if you work, Price, because there was a murder committed here last night.'

They reckoned that someone hit this fellow, he had the skip up on the lorry and they reckon he was hit partly on the back of the head or partly on the back of the neck and then the skip was dropped on to his head. So there was nothing wrong with his body, but his fucking head was flat as a pancake!

And it came on the TV news; they said there's a death on the job, so I said to the foreman, 'Well, I don't work.'

He said, 'Thank you, Pricey, if that's the crack, but if you would like to turn in tomorrow then it's up to you.'

I said, 'I will tomorrow, but it's not on today.'

'Fair enough, I'll leave it to you,' he replied.

I said, 'Sound.'

They reckoned that a former member of the IRA by the name of O'Malley had been murdered when the skip lorry he owned was used as a murder weapon! Somehow, O'Malley's head had been crushed beneath the skip. Although subsequent forensic testing showed no mechanical fault with the skip wagon, it had had its skip lowered, resulting in O'Malley having his head crushed. The only conclusion that the police could come to was foul play by people unknown.

On the M56 job, there was Tommy Malone and I, now the late Tommy Malone. I couldn't get over it when they told me he had died. Billy McGeardy was down there as well; he was foreman of the job down the valley; he was in charge of scrapers.

Malone, John McGeardy, and Tommy Maginty from Macclesfield are very good friends of mine. They are good people, really good people, and they're well known through Britain: any big job, a dam job, motorways, they can do it; they're all known.

This day, when we got laid off from the M56 job, Malone and Johnny English were with me. Russell and me were in digs in the Star Inn, in Stathem Lymm, Cheshire, just off the M6. We didn't have to go into Manchester for anything we needed, it was all local if you wanted anything; there was no shortage of ladies round there either.

This particular day, we were rained off and the boy said to Tommy Malone, John, Johnny English, Russell and me, 'Come up to the market field, it's not far up the road.' There was about two or three carloads of us went up to Macclesfield.

'We've got a good club up there, it's a great old place; you'll like it, it's a good crack,' he said.

I said, 'Sound.'

'Fuck off, and we'll see you in the morning,' the foreman said.

'Come to the transport café, we'll all be waiting in the transport café. You can have a bit of breakfast there or whatever,' I answered.

Jacko, Johnny English and Tommy Malone all went off to Macclesfield. Little Tommy Malone, if you look at him sideways, his nose comes out further than his cheekbones. John McGeardy, who was older than us, was there as well. So anyway, we were all up in Macclesfield and we were all on the fucking beer.

We were in the club before time, before it opened and arms were outstretched welcoming us, 'Come in, come in, boys.' Eventually, we all landed up in John McGeardy's house where we watched a video. By then some of them had wavered by the wayside and everywhere, and at least one was sleeping. We had got to that stage.

So I got in to John McGeardy's house and his missus put out some sandwiches for us and I said, 'No, we're going back out now.' Out of three carloads there were just three of us left standing!

We went to this pub and they couldn't get me off these fucking drums! Malone says to me, 'The next pub we go to, Price, be careful because this fellow, he's a bit of a hard bastard that keeps the pub.' As it turns out, there was no trouble and he served us and we went on our merry way to the next.

Malone said to me, 'Johnny English can stay in my pad for the night, one can doss on the floor and the other one, Eddy, can stay too.'

I said, 'That will do and we'll carry on to work in the morning.'

But the morning never came, did it? We went into a Chinese, we ordered the food and we sat down waiting whilst our order was made up. We'd paid for it and all we wanted was for it to be put on the counter and to carry it away and go home tidy.

The door was barged open and in walked trouble in the guise of four or five Scottish lads, and could they make some noise! They were unruly because they too had had a good skinful of booze; we'd had a good drink and they'd had a good drink ... a lethal Gaelic cocktail!

We sat patiently awaiting our order, and eventually the Chinese lady came through with our carryout in bags. After a good drinking session we were ready to demolish the Great Wall of China, but a takeaway would have to suffice. These Scottish boys, they grab hold of our bags and you know the crack.

I said, 'Excuse me, gentlemen, they are ours, they are paid orders.'

'Och aye, you get the seconds,' was, in an almost incoherent way, thrown out of one of the mouths of the group. I didn't see the funny side of it and Johnny and Malone certainly didn't either, because I could see them getting worked up for a fight and they were walking towards them.

I said, 'Look here, now ...' but before I could finish my words I could see the head of Johnny English going in the direction of a Scottish nose! Scottish blood sprayed everywhere! I thought, this is fucking it, like!

The next thing I know, one of the Scottish lads grabbed a hold of me from the side. I got around that and the other fucker was trying to get me, so I thumped one with a pile driver of a punch and he went fucking down like the *Titanic* and the other one, he could have had me from the side but he was on the down there hugging the fucking floor as well.

But I didn't quite catch him right and he was trying to get back up so I grabbed hold of a chair and, as I swung it behind me to bring it down on his head, I caught the fucking front plate-glass window, and didn't the whole fucking window go in! Oh, fucking hell! The whole shop window went in! I carried on and continued to smash him over the head with the chair anyway.

All the time this was going on, the Chinese woman who served us is shouting something in Chinese at us, probably giving a running commentary to the Chinese workers through the back.

The next thing, there was police, and more fucking police and more police. We didn't have time to go anywhere; the police dogs were there too, everything was there. And out came the fucking truncheons, they didn't think about it.

The police pointed at us and said, 'You two are going in to that van.'

I said to the policeman, who was a sergeant or something, 'I'm not going into any fucking van at all.'

He said, 'You're going in the easy way or the fucking hard way, pal! You can take it or leave it.'

I said, 'Hey, we did fuck all, them's the bastards!'

'You get in that van now,' the policeman ordered.

I didn't see any of the Scots boys getting in there.

Tommy Malone said to me, 'Jesus Christ! There's another car following them again, Price, and another, and another.'

I've never seen so many police, they don't fuck about up there, and all the heavy sticks were out!

And, again, the policeman ordered, 'The hard way or the easy way, it's up to you. I don't care which way you go in.'

As I stepped into the police van, I said, 'When a man's got to go, he's got to go.'

So English and me, we went into the van like sheep. We took the easy way. English, he was shitting himself because they locked us in the cells and we were about four days in police custody in these fucking police cells, old cobbled floors, a right old fucking cow shed of a place. They wanted to put us in together on the one shift and the other shift put us on our own.

I said, 'You know, I told you what fucking happened.'

I was told, 'You're waiting 'til court day.'

It was either three days or four days in police custody together; we missed a shave. Eventually, when the court day started, I was surprised to see the Scots boys were there and they admitted it was their fault. I thought, this is it, we'll walk free, but I was on a bender, a suspended prison sentence for previous assaults! I only had a month or two to go to clear this bender, a six-month bender, and, fuck me, they give me three months on the bender (nine months in all), fucking hell! I had nine months and I landed up in Strangeways Prison, in Manchester.

Thankfully, such confrontations with the police when I was on the road were rare. This other one I want to tell you about was when we ended up in Merseyside, in Birkenhead. We were doing earthmoving for the new dock being built there.

We went across to the pool (Liverpool) one night and, on the way over, we met two ladies who were coming back from the pool and so my mate took one home and I took the other one. I said, 'I'm in digs around the place,' and that was that. Fucking hell, I didn't know if I should have said that. I normally liked to know them well before I fucked them. If you didn't do it, they would think there was something wrong.

Near the dock in Liverpool was the Dorick pub; I used to drink in the Dorick, which is on the main road. I was on the phone one night in a pub near the dock and most of the boys were all over the place, and some of them were in the Dorick.

I was on the phone to my mother this night to see how she was and all that; if she was ever ill then I'd say, 'Don't worry about me, I'll always get home.' That was all I cared about. I was on the phone in the corridor of this pub and there was this fellow: flat nose, cauliflower ear and no neck, he was on crutches, he had done something to his foot and it was in plaster of Paris.

I eyed him up and down, noting that he wasn't a threat, and continued my conversation. 'Yeah,' I said, 'I'm all right, Mam. Yes, we'll be careful, don't worry, don't worry.' You know how mothers worry.

Now this fellow, he hit me along the legs with one of his crutches to get my attention, and he said, 'Phone me a fucking taxi, will you, Taff?'

I said, 'Hold on, can't you see that I'm on the phone, just a second.'

He said, 'I'll see you again!'

I knew I had fucking problems now and I said, 'I'll see you again, all right!'

He was poking me again with one of his crutches! So I quickly said goodbye to my mother and I put the phone down.

'Look, phone me a taxi, Taff!' he growled.

I glared at him and said, 'Phone for your own fucking taxi!'

I thought he was a bit lame and I didn't really want to flatten him, so I said, 'What the fucking hell are you poking me for? You could see I was getting more and more upset because I was talking to my mother and nobody is supposed to bother me because it's special, you fucking round-faced bastard! You ever do that again and I'll whip that fucking stick out of your hands and ram it right up your fucking arse!'

So next thing, he lifted up the crutch and he was going to crack me over the head with it, so I tore into the bastard and down he went. There were two chairs and there was a table, if I can remember. I thought, You deserve a fucking ankle like that, so I hit him right over the fucking head with one of the chairs and I said, 'You fucking old bastard!'

Hearing the ruckus, my mate Peter Schofield came running out. 'Price, they've phoned the police, fucking leg it,' he said.

So I legged it up the road and down the alleyway and

eventually came on to the main road. I thought, I'll go to the Dorick; I'll fuck off now out of the way.

The next thing, round the corner came two squad cars and they had the dogs with them as well, Alsatians. Fuck me, I was up against the wall and they said, 'You'll not move now because they will fucking have you.'

I said, 'Good dog, good dog.'

The next thing, they had me and locked me up. When I was in the station I thought, Fucking hell, not again!

The next day, I was supposed to travel down from Seaforth, as they had finished the job up there; they were taking so many down, and so many were going to another job and so many were going to South Wales on the Morriston by-pass. They were going to be travelling the machines by road and they would get escorted all the way, and they would change from county to county with the police escort.

The next thing, I'm fucking locked up. I thought, I'm going to miss going to fucking Wales now so they might send someone else instead of me. I told the police that this wasn't my fault. The next thing I knew, I thought I could hear Schofield's voice.

The custody sergeant had me brought out from the cell now and, sure enough, it was Peter Schofield. They had him locked up too and it was all over this squashed-nose arsehole on crutches!

Peter told the police that he wasn't at fault and explained how the fellow went to batter him with a stick. After I had done the damage to this arsehole, Peter said, 'Don't worry, Price, don't worry, just get the fuck out of it.'

What did it matter? The police had me. They got me out of the cell and I could see this one policeman having words in the sergeant's ear. I could hear the constable saying to the sergeant, 'Do you know who it was he turned over?'

The sergeant said, 'No!'

So the constable said the name in the sergeant's ear! 'Fucking hell,' the sergeant said. As he raised his eyebrows and started laughing out aloud he said, 'It couldn't have happened to a nicer man!'

I cottoned on to what was going on. Obviously this fellow on crutches was the local Mr Big of the Merseyside Mafia.

I said, 'Hey, give me a break, guys. I'm supposed to be going to South Wales today.'

The sergeant said, 'Price, it's your fucking lucky day, now get your fucking arse out of here, we don't want to see …'

Before he could finish what he was saying, I said, 'I'm away in the morning, anyway.'

He must have been a bad bastard, this Mr Big, if you know what I mean. Once the sergeant heard his name, he was like, 'Fucking hell!' I was lucky that I was let go and only told to fuck off.

With that little crutch incident behind me, we went down to the Morriston by-pass then, and the Moke was there, big Tony Gold; fine-looking fellow. You know in Somerset, where you get men wearing those big bushy side-burns. Well, he was like that, he was a Moke.

There we were, down by the Morriston by-pass and we went into Swansea one night. I was hoping I would see some of the boys there. We walked into this club and I didn't know who was bouncing down there and we didn't have a chance to talk to see who was who and so we walked up to the bar.

'What a fine-looking club this is,' said the Moke.

'Aye,' I said, 'it certainly is.' It was the Sands Club.

We were speaking to a girl behind the bar and I said, 'What time is last orders?'

She took the piss out of us and said, 'About 10 o'clock.'

Well, by this time it was half-past nine, or something like that, and we had a lot of drinking to catch up on.

I said, 'I think you're wrong there. You're not taking the piss out of us, are you?'

She put her arm up and called somebody, and I said, 'She's a cheeky fucker. She's taking the piss. It's not on.'

'Don't look now, there's a bit of a gang coming towards us,' the Moke said.

I looked around and there was a short stocky fellow headed in our direction with about six or seven boys coming up behind him. They were the bouncers and the fellow heading them goes like this and drops his hat. 'Bloody Malcolm Price,' he says.

Wasn't it only Mr Hilliard from London … he was the manager of the club in Merthyr, wasn't he?

'Bloody Malcolm Price,' he said.

I said, 'Mr Hilliard, I've never seen you for years,' and all the girls behind the bar were standing there stunned!

He introduced me to all the bouncers, 'This is Pricey … and when you're coming again, don't leave it so long, and you'll have a meal on the house here.'

Oh, and last orders was well after midnight. The barmaid was taking the fucking piss out of us, wasn't she? She'd nearly started World War Fucking Three!

Wherever you go, there's always one local hero who wants to starts trouble. Whether they wanted to start an innocuous argument or a full man-to-man fight, it just seemed to happen! I recall bumping into one of these local heroes, when I went back to the M56.

Lambert and me went for a drink in the local pub, when this fellow started giving me the evil eye! When you're travelling, some people make out that you shouldn't be in their area, their territory, and we'd say, 'We're only here to do a job, we're not going to get familiar, you know. We're only passing through.'

The fellow said, 'Why don't you go to Warrington? It's a bigger place for you fuckers. Why don't you go there?'

I said, 'We've got good digs here, a lovely landlord and a lovely landlady, the food is good and so is the beer. Have you ever been to a place like that?'

He said, 'No.'

I said, 'Well, you would know fuck all about it then.'

So he was getting mad now – him and me – so I said, 'If you've got any fucking beef, let us fucking go outside, simple as that. So outside now!'

He was willing, so outside 'now' he fucking went and so did the landlord and the entire bar too! They all stood there in a circle as if this was some sort of Saturday night entertainment especially brought in for their pleasure. The entire bar was out, carrying their pints with them too.

I said, 'If you want a fucking go, it's your fucking choice.'

He let one go; it was well telegraphed to me long before his arm started to move and he missed by a mile. I went straight in to him with the hands and I kept punching at him 'til I pounded him down on to the floor and my plan was to put him on to the floor and keep him there.

I was just going to finish him off, but he was out anyway and the landlord said, 'Mal, he's had enough.'

I said, 'So be it.'

These local heroes, each one thought they were the King Kong of the world, but I soon turned each one of them into Mickey Mouse. I'd never throw my weight about intentionally and I'd never bully people, but I always use my right to defend myself.

Anyway, there was Jacko the Cone, who was up at Macclesfield, and he turned up with his gang on the M56; he was in charge of the tracked machines and boxes. In charge of the scrapers was Mickey Lamb, big Mick Lamb. Jacko brought this fucking big fellow, who I hadn't seen before, to the pub; he worked as the foreman on D-8 dozers and boxes (box scrapers) in a different party.

This fellow was tall and broad, but I've never seen such a hairy fellow; he had hairs sprouting out of his collar all around his neck like strands of candyfloss and we called him Tarzan. Fuck me, but the first time he saw me he had a go! He didn't fit in; he was a bit of a bully really.

Trying to be the big hard man he said, 'Are you into arm-wrestling?'

I said, 'I don't do that fucking game. I don't play games like that. I don't do that fucking crack.'

Trying to wind me up he said, 'What can you fucking do then?'

'Oh,' I said, 'I think we'd better go outside, I can feel what's going to happen here and I don't want to lose my digs, like, you fucking bastard! When you come on your own you'll not know you've been born, you fucking ...'

So outside he went, but I gave him a good two minutes on his own when I said, 'Go on, out the back.' I went out after giving him his two minutes, which might have felt like two hours to him. That was my plan, to get him wound up before I went out.

As I approached him, he turned to face me, and in went my boot! I didn't mess about with him, I punched him straight in the mouth and, when he went down, I kicked out his teeth and gone was his award-winning smile; his jaw was broke, too. He stayed down for a while!

I don't know whether Jacko took him to hospital in his car or what. The next day at work, I found out that they must have kept him in hospital overnight or something because the following day he wasn't at work. Jacko must have told someone and it got back, so the site foreman came to me.

Mickey Lamb said, 'What have you done to my foreman, Pricey? You've put him into fucking hospital!'

I said, 'How long is he going to be in?'

He said, 'His job's yours, if you want it. You could be foreman over the boxes [box scrapers].'

'No. I'd rather stick to working the scrapers,' I said.

The next morning, Mad Mick and me were parking up the car at the site compound and as we got out we could sense something in the air. The big fellow, Tarzan, I'd put into hospital, well, it turned out he got out earlier than I thought. We didn't know that he was waiting round the corner, not until Mick said, 'The big fellow's around the corner, Price.' He'd got to the corner before me and could see what was going on.

I said, 'Fair enough.'

I walked around and the rest of the fellows stopped behind me. Tarzan, the hairy gorilla, stood his ground. I could see that he had a heavy bar in his hand that he was going to use to smash my skull in.

I went up to him and said, 'Look! You have two options here. You can walk away or, if I get hold of the bar, I'm going to beat you first, break every bone in your body and then I'm going to park the bar up by shoving it up your arse.' You know what he did, he just threw the bar down and he walked away.

I thought that was the end of that, but the following day, Tarzan's missus was at the site looking for me with a machete! Yes, she came the next day with a big machete because little Malone came up to me the next day and told me what had happened.

Her plan was to catch me in my car whilst stopping at a set of nearby traffic lights, and if the lights had gone against me then she was going to take this machete out of the hiding place in the pram she was pushing and serve me up good and proper with it! Fancy, a woman going to do a man's work.

Eventually, when I came back to Merthyr, there was a new company and I joined Wimpey on the M4 in South Wales.

The foreman asked, 'What do you want, Price, do you want a TS 24?'

I replied, 'Yes, a 24 will do me fine, Sam.'

As I walked on the job this one morning, which was now completely different from when they had all sorts on the job and when they were working on the M4, who should be there but Tarzan. Without further ado, he just made his way to the car and he jacked in the job on the spot. The foreman said, 'I assume you're a mate of Tarzan, Price?' He wasn't kidding me, he knew about it. I never saw Tarzan again after that.

Trouble wouldn't just come from local heroes or fellow workers. We went down from Sheffield to the opencast at Blaenavon, where the big pit is. It's still open to the public, but it's right up in the mountains. We went to a pub called the Rifleman. That's where a double murder was committed. Just before we got there, two fellows were killed in the cottages behind the Rifleman. There were police everywhere. That was when I started working for Wimpey as a young boy; that was when all the young lads were working on the open roads just before they started going up country and looking for work elsewhere. I went up country after that.

I remember there was a double-decker bus outside the house. Back then, the buses were old ones with big long bonnets on the front. There was this conductor who I dragged right out of his seat because he was blasting the horn of the bus! I was done for common assault. But I was just trying to get some sleep as I was working nights for Wimpey and he was tooting this bloody horn outside.

Obviously, I've had some fights in my time, and I don't rate anyone in particular as being the hardest I've ever come up against, either in the ring or out of it. I've faced some hard bastards and all I can say is it's lucky that I caught them, because, if they had got hold of me, I think they would have thrown me about like a tennis ball.

A normal fighter in the street fights in a different way from a disciplined boxer. A boxer can throw a six-inch punch. A six-inch punch can knock you clean down. I'm very wary of those boxers, I can tell you. If you get a boxer that can street fight and he mixes it together then it makes a lethal combination! I mixed boxing and street fighting into a cocktail and when I knocked them down I kept them down by use of the boot.

I haven't any recollections of who was the hardest or what was the most violent fight I've been involved in. One of the strangest fights, though, was when we were up in North Wales once. When we arrived I fought in the boxing booths up there because I was a bit short on ready cash.

I remember it was at Menai Bridge Fair; a big showground that went on for a week, all through the streets. It wasn't far from St Asaph. I was working there with a few lads from Merthyr. We were driving SN 35 dump trucks on the M6.

I was a bit skint and we were all a bit short on cash, really, due to the weather being so bad. We were rained off every day and this was about the time when the boss was due to lay us off anyway, because when the bad weather comes in the winter, they finish you then and restart you in the spring. You can't use earthmoving equipment when it's really wet, as they get bogged down. When anyone got married, we'd call that being bogged down too!

The general foreman for McAlpine, a little Irish fellow – I forget his name now; a hell of a boy he was, he said, 'A big lad like you, you should be up there at the Menai Fair having a go earning yourself an extra few bob for the beer.'

Old Billy Laing, Colin Garcia, Shinco and me, Shinco was my corner lad – we went up to the fair looking for the boxing booth. We went into this old shamble and the showman asked if anyone wanted to go in the ring to fight one of his men. I put my hand up and he said, 'Here's a new lad who wants it.'

I fought this black lad and the booth owner said he'd give me so much if I went three rounds and if I knocked him out I'd get a bit more. I was offered so much per round if I stuck the pace with him. So anyway, they gave me an old pair of trunks that were nearly hanging off me and they give me an old pair of daps, which just about fitted me, and then off I went into the ring.

I was a bit ring-rusty. These lads boxing in the booths are training every day and they are there all the time. You had to expect the rough and tumble in the first round. As soon as I got into the ring I said to the boys, 'Give me a drop of water.' They were my corner men.

'Water! He wants water,' one of them said.

I thought, I'm not going to get my water now. They finally found the water but no bucket; they couldn't find the bucket! I said, 'Look under the ring.' This was a pantomime waiting to happen, it was a good laugh.

The late Billy Laing came up now and he was a hell of a boy himself and he said, 'Do your best, Pricey and let's get back to the pub.'

I said, 'I'll do the best job I can, although I'm a bit rusty, but I'll get into the flow of things.' As soon as I put my hands up and he saw the way my hands were, they knew that I had been in the ring before.

We had the rough and tumble I expected to have in the first round. I couldn't find my distance and I was out of line with the firepower. The second round, I caught him tidy: down he goes. When he went down I was standing with the ref. He was the owner of the money roll and he kept pushing me back and I went right back into my corner.

The ref hadn't started the count; Billy Laing counted up to 50 and I counted up to 100 and he's still trying to push me and I said, 'I can't go anywhere else, I'm up against the ropes in the neutral corner,' but he was stalling so as to let his man get up.

He said, 'You stay there, you fucking bastard.'

I said, 'Get off me and start the count.'

By now, Billy Laing had counted to 200, and then he had to get up then, didn't he? The ref was saying to his man, 'How many fingers can you see?' and all that, and he was stalling for more time. Anyway, he gave me so much money and fuck knows what.

I said, 'Just give me the money; I just want to get out of here while the pub's still open.'

He said, 'You bastard, I could have done with you earlier in the season. What's your name?'

I said, 'Pricey from Merthyr.'

He said, 'I'll remember that.'

I hadn't been training for a long time, but it was a good crack. That probably goes down as one of the longest fights I've ever had because fights don't last for too long, not on the road.

Someone once asked me if I knew the feeling of fear. Oh, I knew fear. Well, really speaking I never feared any fucker at that time; I've got to be honest. But I knew fear, the fear of losing! There was never any fear of combat! My father instilled that fear into me and that was what drove me on to win ... the fear of what was to come after you went home saying you'd lost! After that, no matter how many I faced, I didn't have any fear.

There's a dancehall in Taunton, off the M5, and we went to see Peter Schofield there one night. My mates were already inside, so Russ Crawford and me went to join them. Schofield heard the bouncers say, 'Take their money and we'll chuck them out. There's four or five of us; and we could just throw them back out again.'

So Schofield told me this. When I went in I said to the bouncers, 'If you don't mind, I'm staying. You and that other cock-eyed fellow, you're going out,' and I put the fucking two of them out.

Although every pub had its bruiser waiting for me, I didn't expect what was waiting to happen to me when I was in company in this pub in Kendal. A few people were playing darts in the Angel pub and we were in listening to the jukebox. The place was about three-quarters full and there was a fellow at the bar I didn't know. I went up for drinks and, with that, he caught me with his elbow and I spilled the drinks. He said, 'I'm sorry.'

I said, 'You've spilled my drinks. You're lucky you don't have to fucking pay for them.'

The next thing, he had me in a fucking headlock and he had me bent over and his other two fogies, who'd been playing darts, made up the numbers to three.

I didn't know this fellow, but now he had me in some sort of a fucking armlock! As a boxer, you need space to perform, but the minute someone gets you close in and starts working your body over, then it becomes a bit more difficult. I've never been held so tight in all my life and I thought, fuck me, this guy's strong!

As I was held, this fellow's mates started putting the boot into me! They were kicking me up the arse and kicking my ribs, and this fellow, he had me fucking tight! I had to improvise; boxing had to go out of the window and the only thing I could do was to reach for his balls! I just grabbed hold of them and I really fucking well had him and he let me go. With his eyes watering, he said, 'Fuck that.'

I was suddenly, and gratefully, released from his iron grip and I reached for a glass, smashed it off a table and sliced the bastard who had hold of me across the face. As chunks of flesh went flying across the room, I yelled, 'Who else wants to pay a visit to the hospital?'

He screamed, 'So, it's like that is it, with a glass?'

I told him, 'I'm outnumbered here, so it is.'

I just laid into him, two-handed, and I kept on fucking him, and those two boys who had been kicking me just stepped back out of it. I kept hitting him through the pub, out the door and into the alley and then he went down, and he went fucking down big time! I followed up by putting the fucking boot in to him. Turns out that he was a professional wrestler, and the bar was a local haunt used by these guys.

You know what the cheeky bastard said when he was in hospital? 'I could have killed him when I locked his head; he's lucky to be fucking alive.'

This man was a professional wrestler and he used to wrestle in the Town Hall in Kendal on a Saturday afternoon. The cheeky bastard, though, also had the cheek to say that I could have killed him as well. That was over, and that was it and I knew he was a strong fucker. I've never had an armlock or headlock like that before.

I remember the first night up in Kendal. We moved into the digs at the Dunn Horse pub, and I didn't want to cause any trouble in the bar. There was this fellow who started some trouble, when we rubbed shoulders at the bar. I said to him, 'I'll see you outside.' He went storming outside and I thought he had gone to wait for me. I said to the boys, 'I won't be two minutes.'

My pal said, 'Pricey, don't do anything to cause trouble; they might throw us out of the digs.'

I said, 'I'll do it outside, don't worry.'

I marched off down the alleyway outside but he wasn't there. I thought the bastard had legged it off home. I went back into the bar and made a quick call in the toilet.

When I got inside, as I was standing having a piss into the urinals, I could hear this toilet going.

The next thing, I kicked the shithouse door open and gave him the surprise of his life when I caught him pulling his trousers up, so I did him over with his trousers down. From the look on his face, you'd have thought he'd shit himself for a second time. I knocked him all over the shithouse. He was all over the shithouse pan and everything! I went back into the bar, but the guy I'd just turned over never came back in.

The confrontations from fellow workers would, at times, happen over the stupidest of reasons and the silliest little arguments, but the pressure of being on the road would often magnify these arguments.

At 6ft 4in and 18 stone, big Glen Rose was the hardest in Kendal. But this day he said the wrong thing to me. He was a nice man, but I think he wanted to have a go at me from the start. He did a whole lot of bouncing in the bowling alley at Morecambe and a few dances up there besides, but he had said something to me early on.

Mike Mahoney and a few boys had come up to see me when I was working on the M6. We were still in digs in Kendal, a pub called the Dunn Horse, and nice people were keeping it (Ken and Ruby). They were good to us and we were good to them. And big Glen went and started it all when he said to me, 'Why are you here during a holiday, then? You don't care much about your family if you're staying here!'

I said, 'That's the wrong fucking thing to say to me about how I care about my family!'

He said something else and I lost it completely; he shouldn't have said that. I lost the fucking head altogether and the red mist came over me. The place was a rough old dive of a place and they shut the doors on the pub and moved the tables back. He made for me, the fucking big bear, and I made for him. Glen had a good set of teeth. *Bonk!* I gave him a straight right! His fucking teeth went one way and his fucking jaw went the other way and that was the end of it. I just wanted one fucking dig at him.

By the time he was down, I was giving him another going over with the boots as well, just to make sure the job was done properly. Mahoney carried Glen upstairs to clean him up, but Glen had shit himself. Mahoney picked him up and, as he did so, managed to get shit all over his hand! Mahoney said, 'Price, here, get hold of him, you can carry him.'

I said, 'We're like Burke and fucking Hare!'

Anyway, Glen was taken upstairs and cleaned up. I was looking around the place and the old dartboard that had a tyre around it had three or four of Glen's teeth that were lying on the ledge.

The thing is, Glen and I became fucking good mates afterwards. But there was no need for what he said he shouldn't have done that and attacked the integrity of my family. That's one thing I never forgave him over; families are very dangerous territory.

He shouldn't have said what he did, but I still had the decency, after he was cleaned up, to put him in his own fucking car and run him to his door and walk back – I left his car with him.

When I dropped him off, his wife said, 'Who did this to him?'

I said, 'I did, with my hands, but he'll tell you he did this and that, but it was his fault.'

I remember the next day, Sunday morning, I went down to the pub with Shinco, Ginger Harris, Mike Mahoney and a few of the boys where Glen used to go on a Sunday morning, and he was there sitting down with three or four of his mates.

I walked up to Glen and said, 'Glen, you can either have a pint or fucking go outside if you want me to finish what you started.'

He said, 'Pricey, I was in the wrong. I'll have a pint.'

We shook hands and that was it; I never carried a grudge.

There was a big fight in the Angel after that, where these bastards broke Colin Garcier's leg and put him in hospital. The first man to say, 'I'm going to find these bastards,' was Glen Rose, because they put a little Scots fellow in hospital as well.

This was a long time ago: the Scots boy used to work for this company called Cataplant from Scotland, and he was a nice fellow and I liked his company. He was in a bad way; they put the boots into him.

The next morning, Glen said, 'We'll come back,' and he parked up the road and said, 'Jump in and we'll go and find these bastards now.'

Glen and me went looking for these fellows who put these two in hospital. We thought Garcier would be lame for the rest of his life because the bone in his leg had come through the other side, making it a compound fracture.

And most of the lads were back at work and they were pulling the trucks up. There were five trucks still stood there and I said to the foreman, 'Where's these bastards that drive these fucking trucks because they put two fucking gentlemen fucking inside and they're mates of ours?'

Big Glen got hold of him and the foreman fucking shit himself. 'What men? I don't want to be involved in this fucking thing; they've jacked and fucked off. Look there's five fucking trucks stood here. They knew better and fucked off,' he said. They'd gone and, in time, Garcier's leg went back to normal and everything.

Sometimes, being on the road, you got to make real good friends with some of the fellows. This was the case when I was Best Man at Barry Peel's wedding. He called in to see me recently; he was on long distance and he had just come back from somewhere in Devon. He's a fucking case, he is. He landed up here and before that he was driving a power crane. He ended up getting a job up my way driving on the M6 because his job was finishing.

He was a machine man himself, he used to drive the machines; and so he got this lass up here in the family way and said, 'Price, could you help me out?'

I said, 'What do you want me to do?'

He said, 'Will you be Best Man when I get hitched?'

I said, 'Aye, too fucking true. I'll help anybody.'

'Thanks, Price, you're doing me a big favour,' he said.

I said, 'Where've you been kipping?'

He said, 'I've been kipping in the shed.'

He married a local girl and he did well for himself and a hell of a nice girl she was too. And his daughter grew up and passed cap and gown at university, and all that, and he was right proud.

The next time he called in at Merthyr, I thought he was all settled and he took up a long-distance lorry driving job and he used to call at the Merthyr Labour Club to see us when he was passing through this way.

He had a lovely home – a beautiful family and a beautiful wife – but his marriage broke up. He said, 'If you're ever passing through Kendal, call in at my local ...' I've forgotten the name of the pub. I think he was actually living at the car park in a caravan the last time he was here.

Christ, he's back to square one now, unless he's back to his wife. But after all that, and all these years, he's back in a bastard caravan, do you know what I mean? But I hope he's back together with the missus now because he's a real character he is. He was one of the best friends you could ever have.

Just over the bridge in Rhyl is a pub, and one night Colin Garcier, old Bill, big young Peter and me went there. There was a dance and a big fight broke out, it frightened people off! Everybody was fighting everybody else. There was fellows throwing punches, so we joined in. There were only a certain amount of us left standing at the end because just about everyone was on the floor! I was stood in the centre of the hall and was punching them out as fast as they came at me, and every time I hit someone, they went down.

I never saw a pub so fucking wrecked. Fuck me, everybody was lying all over the place and there was a woman who came into the pub and she was lifting the men's heads up by their hair because she was looking for her husband; fuck me, it was comical! And the landlord, he was just fucking amazed. He'd never seen that amount of people laid out before.

Well, fucking hell, I wouldn't like to say how many were on the floor that night; there were only a few standing over the far end, that was it. It was a free for fucking all. The thing is, as you're fighting one fucker, you might turn around and you would be fighting another fucker. A hard night's fighting followed a hard night's drinking.

After a hard day at work breathing in the dust of the site, there was nothing better to do than go out drinking. There really weren't that many drugs around. Fuck me; I didn't even know that you could buy Aspirin across the counter, that's how naïve I was.

We were on the M56 and they promised to pick this boy and me up. We were going by the M56 and this blond lad – his father was manager of a pit somewhere down west – had a hell of a life over drugs and I wonder if he's still alive now. He called at my digs to pick me up to go for a drink. I was at the bar having a pint and talking to the landlord and they said, 'Here's your mate, Pricey.'

He said, 'We'll go in to Warrington.'

'All right,' I said.

And into the Jag we went, and as I got in he said, 'Hey, Price.' As I looked at him, he leaned over and put his hand towards my mouth. 'Pop this on your tongue,' he said, as I willingly stuck my tongue out.

I said, 'What's this? Is it as good as that smoke you give me down the road on the other job?'

'Oh, yeah, you'll get a good giggle on this,' he said.

I said, 'It's not fucking bad, is it?'

'No, just drop it down and swallow it,' he said.

About twenty minutes later, we were in this big country pub with a a great jukebox and all the old records, everything on we wanted. The beer was good and there was a restaurant through the French windows and everything was there; it was a lovely summer night.

The next thing, we're talking away and the boy is having a smoke and having a good old laugh and I seemed to glance now at this jukebox and it was a colourful jukebox all right. I was all right until the jukebox started to breathe. He, ho! I thought, No!

I took another sip and I said, 'Whose round is it?' But all that came out was: 'Ooooh, oooh.' I knew what I wanted to say, but I couldn't and they all burst out fucking laughing and they asked what was the matter. I said, 'Ooooh.' I sounded like a fucking old gramophone playing at slow speed and, when I looked at the fucking jukebox again, it seemed bigger. Fucking hell, I thought I was going off my head! Every time I went to talk they were laughing so much, these bastards. Now the other four or five that were with me knew the crack, it was the tablet, wasn't it? And I didn't know anything about the effects of acid.

The landlord came up and said, 'I've seen the carry on.'

I stood up and said, 'We haven't done anything, like, and, if we have, I'll apologise,' but what actually came out of my mouth was, 'Whooowholll,' it was exactly like that. We had to go because it was that or the police.

Then they were laughing like fucking clowns. It was the weirdest sensation I've ever had! The hairs on the back of my neck were standing up and I couldn't talk. I wondered how long this was going to last. I was trapped in a hallucinogenic world! I was certainly up a height with Lucy in the Sky with Diamonds (LSD).

I was really making an arsehole of myself and it was a tablet of acid and I didn't know this, but the others did. 'Oh,' I said, 'is someone playing with the lights, like?' Well, nobody was playing with the lights; it was a car and we were on the road, and it was dark and the lights were just passing by.

When I went into the digs, I was that afraid and paranoid. I looked under the bed and in the wardrobe. In fact, I looked in the wardrobe two or three times. I was not fucking getting into that bed. Fucking hell, I thought, I don't want to experience this any more and so I sat with my back on the pillow and thought I'd better leave the lights on. Fucking hell! I had never been like that in my life. I thought, when am I going to get out of this? Perhaps I'll stay like this forever! I was a bit panicky, but I couldn't talk.

The following day, it cleared up, but I was shaking. I had the shakes and I lost my head with the young fellow who gave me the acid. He said, 'Did you have a bad trip, Price?'

'Don't you ever give me that stuff again. It would turn a man off his fucking head. I don't want any more of that fucking shit,' I said.

He said, 'I'm sorry, Price, I should have warned you, sometimes you go on a good one, but you had a bad one.'

There was a voice in the back of my head; I could hear

breathing, 'Ahaaaaaa.' You know you don't fucking hear anything like that. I didn't like it and it frightened me to death for hours.

That was the closest thing I have experienced to what I could say was fear. I couldn't go to sleep for hours, as I was afraid to shut my eyes. It's not my stuff at all. So now you can see what it does for you from that experience. I can't understand why anybody likes to take this stuff; there's no enjoyment in taking drugs.

That was my time on the road. They were mad, crazy, nutty, round the bend, foolish, barmy, bizarre experiences and encounters, but I had great times and have great memories of the lads I worked with.

CHAPTER 8

VIOLENCE

A good mate of mine, Ernie Arnold, and me were both in the same game, and we started about the same time. We've been mates for a long time; as we had worked together in the past.

I used to spar with Ernie, and I was also chief sparring partner with Chick Calderwood, British Cruiserweight Champ and contender for the World Championship Crown. I was proud of all the fellows in the gym I met, especially little Gerald Jones.

Ernie Arnold came up from Pontypridd; he was having trouble with a lot of locals down there and this and that. There's never been a lot of trouble in Pontypridd, I might have had a few nights in a dancehall down there, but we never had any trouble from the area where Tom Jones comes from and everyone is working class and everybody gets along.

We went down to help Arnold out with this trouble he was having and he said, 'Bring a couple of fellows with you.'

I asked, 'How many is there?'

He said, 'There's about eight of them.'

We went down on the Saturday to help him. He didn't say what it was over and, anyway, you have to understand that every town and every village has got their own hard man.

When we were in there, a fight broke out and Arnold was on the floor rolling about with one or two blokes. I stuck my leg out and tripped one of them over. Arnold and this other fellow, the two of them, were still on the floor rolling around. He was on the way up off the floor so I dragged this other one away and they fucked off through the door. I smacked one of these fellows and he went out cold.

I wondered what it was all about; there was more to this trouble Arnold had than he was letting on! The next thing, I was down there and I was working for Murphy's, not Murphy the Lefter, this was Spud Murphy's earthmoving firm. He was working on this earthmoving job for some favours and sometimes he himself would be on motor scrapers.

There was this old fellow, I can never remember his name, but he was well known around South Wales. He could drive cranes; he could drive anything, but he's now gone. One of the old guys, you know. Anyway, we got rained off on a Saturday morning and we had to stop.

We went straight on the piss, straight from work on the lash. I was driving the car and he wanted to get to

Pontypridd. I couldn't see him catch the train to Ponty so I ran him down there and we had a few pints again. I was pissed going down.

We ended up in a pub. I went in and was talking to Arnold and this and that and I don't know where the old fellow went; he didn't live far, just up the road from Pontypridd. So I had words with somebody, or somebody had words with me, and I forget what it was. Even though I'd had a drink, I saw four or five fellows and I didn't know who was who; someone pushed me or something and I heard, 'Pricey! Pricey!' It was Arnold's voice; what the fuck did he want? I went to have a look, but I didn't get far. I didn't know it at the time, but Arnold had stuck a fucker on me and so the next thing I knew I was on my hands and knees trying to get up. Then it happened. They were kicking at me from all sides and they did a really first-class job on me with their feet-mucking job, couldn't have done better myself.

I mean, you never do that to a fucking friend, do you? I was half-cut and my guard was down because I was with a friend. They didn't have much resistance from me. You don't go into a friend's place and have a drink and expect that to happen. I was well and truly done over, and for what? I had to give it a week or two now for my patched-up ribs to get working again; I couldn't even cough! They really did a good fucking job on me, I can tell you.

But, I thought to myself, he is going to see me again, I can assure you. I said to Mike Mahoney, 'They're healed up a bit now, it's been about a fortnight and they don't feel so bad.'

I was going to have to get back to fitness if I was going to give Arnold the return visit. I did a bit of running up and down and did a bit of work in Tredegar and I was ready to go back down to Arnold's pub in Pontypridd.

I saw Mike Mahoney and said, 'I want to ask you a favour. I'm going to have a go with Arnold; I'm going to do this bastard! What he did to me isn't on! Will you come and watch my back?' Mike, being a true friend, agreed. Willy Watson and Mahoney said, 'We'll go down with you.'

I said, 'Just watch my back, that's all I want you to do. I don't want you to get into any problems, just watch my back.'

They said, 'That sounds right.'

So down we went and we saw a couple of fellows from Merthyr who were living down there at this time. One fellow and his mate said, 'The police are walking around today, Price. They are out in force today, like.' Obviously, someone had given them the tip-off.

I said, 'Oh, aye.'

He said, 'They'll be watching you, Price, so watch it.'

I said, 'Sound, thank you for the advice.'

Into the pub we went, and Arnold's girlfriend was there along with her mother; at least I think it was her mother. So, in between this, I learned that it was Arnold who had slung one on me and I found out that it was his girlfriend's brother who was the one to put the boots into my ribs.

We walked into the bar and she didn't know what to do, his girlfriend.

I asked her, 'Is Ernie here?' I thought we'd go outside and it would be one-to-one and that would be fucking it.

She said, 'He's not here, Malcolm. He's in Cardiff.'

I had already told her, 'I've come down to do your fucking boyfriend.' That's the exact words I spoke to her.

We thought he was waiting upstairs, but at that point a police sergeant turned up with a white-collar job with pips on his shoulder at his side.

The top-ranking policeman said, 'Are you Malcolm?'

I said, 'Yes.'

He said, 'This is not a social call. Malcolm, we are going to ask you once and not twice, leave town now because we know what you're here for.'

I said, 'If you remember, I said it was like I said and I'd like to settle up a score.'

He said, 'Not in this town you're not and not today you're not and, as far as I'm concerned, it's not going to happen in this town. We are here for that or we lock you up now.'

So I said to Mike, 'Let's go.'

We drank in every pub and ended up going to the Rhonda to see Bangy. Now Bangy looks more like a fighter than the actor Charles Bronson himself. He's a ripe old fucker and he was a good boxer; he was also in the gym. I was telling him about the police and how the bastards told me to get away when I would have waited 'til Arnold got back from Cardiff.

Bangy said, 'Let's go back and finish the bastard.' Well, the poor bugger has had half of his stomach taken away; he looks a hard bastard and he is a hard bastard.

I said, 'No trouble, you're not getting worried with my fucking problems.'

A couple of months after that, Arnold had left, apparently, and went abroad. Spain. After he had fucked off out of the country. I didn't see him for years. The next time I saw him was at Eddie Thomas's funeral in 1997.

After Arnold disappeared, I saw Eddie Thomas. I used to go down to the house to see him when he was ill. I went to see how he was and he said, 'I don't want any of the boys fighting between each other, that's not the way I trained them, not for any of this.'

I said, 'It wasn't my fault, Ed. I went down first to help him out when he was in trouble!'

He said, 'I want none of you fighting between yourselves. Please, give me your word.'

I said, 'There will be no problem on my part; it's wearing off now anyway.'

He said, 'Give me your word, I want your word. I don't want my boys fighting among themselves, it would be wrong and I won't have it. You don't want to fight him.'

A few years had passed and that's when I saw Arnold at Eddie's funeral and he was waiting outside the house. I walked in and thought, this isn't the place and time you should be saying anything about things like that.

I was walking back and the big bastard caught up with me.

I said, 'You big bastard!' He's tall, see.

'Pricey,' he said, 'I'm sorry.'

I said, 'The smile was there all the time.'

What Arnold did to me, I don't do that to friends and I don't expect it from them, especially when I stuck my chin out for him.

VIOLENCE

There have been times when I've been accused of certain things I didn't do. In one incident down in Kilgetty, the police roped me in for something I didn't know anything about – attempted murder!

What made them believe I was the man responsible for this crime, I don't really know. When I was at the police station there was this CID fellow who was interrogating my friend and me and he said, 'Look, it once took six of us to lock this man up one night and it was hard work, so we know it wasn't some little fairy who did this damage to him.'

I said, 'Yes, but what has it to do with me?'

He said, 'I know all these locals from here to Lands End and you are the only fellow who was staying here at that time who was capable of causing such injuries to a man like him.'

I said, 'I still don't know what you're on about.'

Apparently a man who was a member of the Special Forces, the SAS or something similar, had been made a right dog's dinner of and put into hospital. Because it was suspected a weapon had been used, I got the suspicion pinned on to me because of what I could do with my hands. The incident was supposed to have happened near Tenby.

The night before this man had been attacked, I was in a nightclub, the Sands Club, in Saundersfoot. I'd been in the proximity of a fight that had taken place in the Sands and, because of this, speckles of blood were splashed on to my coat.

I don't know whether any of the blood went over my

mate Peter or not, but this policeman thought that this blood had something to do with this thing and obviously he thought I must have had something to do with it, but it wasn't me; a fight actually happened right by the side of us in the Sands that night and that is where the blood that was on my jacket came from.

They, the police, took it that this blood might have come from the victim, so they sent all of our clothes for forensic reports. We were bailed to go back six to eight weeks later. At that time, I was working away from home on the motorways and Peter was working somewhere else. I only went down to see Peter; we're old friends and had worked on the M5 together at Taunton, and I'd met him in Seaforth, Liverpool. I could have faced an attempted murder charge, but then the police let me out.

I said nothing about it, simple as that. Then the police were on about this fellow and I said, 'Which fellow? I don't know who you're on about, I'm not from here, anyway.'

But he insisted that I had something to do with it because of the record I had. He said, 'You're the only fellow around here that could have done a man like him in such a way.'

We had to go back in six weeks and we were then cleared because the forensic reports were in our favour – the blood found on us wasn't that of the victim.

I let myself go in this next incident; I'd been drinking every day for weeks. I was in the King's Arms pub in Merthyr and I had a little argument. I've always been a heavy drinker and when I was younger I could handle it, but I didn't realise I was getting older, and it started to take its toll, but the thing is I couldn't handle it like I used to.

I broke the code, because when I asked a fellow out or somebody offered me out, I'd always make sure they walked before me, but when the landlord asked, 'Boys, I'm going to have to ask you to leave,' I walked first, like a fucking clown, and I didn't have my wits about me that day because I was pissed. I should have walked out behind the boys, but I didn't! The next thing, I went outside and I had my T-shirt pulled over my head. By the time I got the T-shirt off, he had his kick in to me and I fell back. I went off the kerb and hit my bastard head on the ground and, before I could say or do anything, I was trying to get back up. The next thing he did was put his full weight on me. Then he bit the end of my nose clean off! I didn't even feel the bite. He must have had sharp teeth!

I went to that place in Newport; they're marvellous down there. I had to go down to Chepstow and they took a little bit off here and there and it's marvellous what they can do. It doesn't look half as bad as it did.

Between you and me, I felt like killing the bastard, but I had second thoughts. What was going through my mind was to leave it for a few years until everyone had forgotten about it, then fucking strike back.

There was one case of GBH that I got away with. Two fellows from Brecon ended up in hospital and one was pretty ill. With me there was big Lynn and Flunky Lewis, and we had some trouble with the guys outside and I ended up with a tool and they were pretty bad, I know that.

I was facing some heavy charges. The only way I could get out of that was if I went for psychiatric treatment. I did two years probation. I had to keep seeing the shrink; I heard that was the only thing that would get me off! I'm going back a long time here! So I did go for psychiatric treatment and that was the only thing that got me off the GBH grief I had in Brecon.

Because of that, I know that there is someone up there looking after me. Another incident in which I was looking at a three to five stretch started when Mansil and me were up in Swansea Road and we had big Gerald in the back of the car, with his broken leg.

When Mansil got out of the car, there was this fellow running alongside him beating the shit out of him with a long stick and I couldn't see who it was. I had been on the beer, a lot of beer. So the next thing I did was run on and Mansil is going down now, he's going down on one knee. I didn't know what this violence was over.

This man was setting about Mansil with what looked liked a long-handled brush. It was like a walking stick with a brush handle and a hook on it. I got out of the car to intervene and became involved in the confrontation. With Gerald Morgan having a leg injury, he couldn't get out of the car.

I said, 'Whoa!' The man let go of me and I put my hand up to defend a blow from the stick that was coming towards my head. It snapped on my hand, the hook went flying and the man then did a runner.

Mansil said, 'I think that was Carl Preese.'

This man, Carl Preese, had been brought up with me when we were living by the tram road when I was a boy. He was younger than me.

I ran Mansil Murphy to the hospital. If I hadn't stopped him, he would have killed Mansil. If that hook had been facing the right way and not the way that it was, he could have gone, he would have been gone. I just saw one of the boys in trouble and that's what I did.

I asked Mansil what it was all about, but I couldn't get head nor tail out of him. I never had any problems with Carl Preese; he was a big lad, but he was always nice to me, as I knew him from a kid and I knew his mother and father. I was sorry that I fell out with him then, but, thinking back to the attack, I thought he was going to do me in.

We went to drop Mansil off, and he said, 'Preese will be tooled up now.'

I said, 'I'm going to knock on his door now.'

He said, 'Pricey, he'll be all tooled up. I'm telling you, he'll have fucking picked something up.'

I said, 'I'll take a knife with me just in case.'

I had bought a very large Bowie knife. I remember showing it to a good friend of mine, Gareth 'Jonah' Jones. I opened the dash of the car and pulled the knife out.

Jonah said, 'That's the biggest knife I've seen in my life!'

I christened the knife, which I'd bought for a particular reason, Wicked Wanda. There was a groove running all the way down the blade, and I said to Jonah, 'That's so the blood can run off the blade.'

I knocked at Preese's door and the light came on and I could see something in this fellow's hand behind the door. The 'something' looked remarkably like a hatchet! What I didn't know was that his wife and kids were in there with him. So that was a bad crack. I said, 'Come out from in there and put your fucking tools down and we'll have a go.' I still didn't know that his wife was in there – if I had, I wouldn't have done what I did.

I stuck the Bowie knife through the door and started hacking away with the knife around the lock area. Council doors aren't much cop, so I kicked what was left of the door open with ease and there he was, on the top of the stairs, standing holding an axe in hand!

When you see a big fellow at the top of the stairs, it takes a bit of working out how you're going to get him. He was taller than me and about the same build.

He said, 'I'll chop your fucking head off if you come up here!'

I said, 'I'll chop your fucking cock off!'

I was foolish enough to try and get up there, wasn't I? There was barking and I saw a Corgi dog and, next thing, I was stunned! I didn't go down, but I just shook my head and blood came off me! I could feel it creeping down my neck as it oozed out of my head and I was going a bit dizzy. I retreated down the stairs, but just before that I heard the kids crying and I said to Preese, 'What's up, like?'

He said, 'I've got my wife and kids here.'

I said, 'I wouldn't have fucking done that to a dog. I wouldn't have done that to anybody, not kids, you know I wouldn't hurt any kids!'

Anyway, it had happened and Mansil Murphy took Wicked Wanda off me. The next thing, the police are at Murphy's house.

They banged me up and demanded to know where the knife was.

I said, 'I didn't have a knife.'

The police again demanded to know. 'Where's the big knife you had, Price?'

Mansil had hidden it. The next day, the police brought me out of the cells, cuffed. They took me back to Murphy's house and the police said, 'If we have to take this flat apart, we will. We want that knife.'

So it wasn't Murphy that gave him the knife; I gave it by telling them where it was. I breached my curfew not to go on to Swansea Road; I was on remand for three months before the case started. My solicitor said that Preese had a cracked skull and all that, so I was facing three to five years!

The time I took that bash to the head with the axe, luckily, I didn't go down. I don't know how, but I felt dizzy, and I was leaking blood from all the bad places, but I didn't go down, despite losing blood at a fast pace.

The doctor said that it would heal itself up and this policewoman said, 'Pricey, I can see your skull, you've got to go to the hospital.'

That's when they took me up there and gave me things to see if my skull was all right.

I had already breached a curfew order imposed by the courts ordering me to stay away from Carl Preese's house. This stemmed from trouble I was giving Preese over the original attack Preese carried out against Mansil. So, by returning to Preese's home armed with a knife, I compounded the charges against me by breaking this curfew and the barrister said, 'Expect three to five years for this, Price.'

So it was a miracle that they only give me nine months and I had already done three so I only had six months to go. I had nine months; but it was my own fault. I didn't comprehend the consequences and this and that and it was too late; what was done was done and that's it.

I remember the policeman who was dealing with the incident said, 'Look, Price, you've come near to it this time. You've done all what you've wanted to do. You're one of the last of the breed in this town, don't you know that now? Pull yourself together and leave these youngsters alone, they are nothing like you or how you've been, Price. Just retire gracefully.'

I remember when I was being taken from the courts and going down to the prison; taking me down to Swansea prison was Sergeant Alan Howells and the police driver. I was on remand for the first incident against Preece. I was the only prisoner in the meat wagon and I'd had a good drink the night before, as I knew I was going down.

We just got outside of Swansea and I felt the sweats coming over me from the drink I had the night before. I said, 'I'm going to spew, honestly! I'm bad after the beer; I'm going to spew. I don't want to spew in the back of the van.'

'Ah, fucking hell, there's only two of us here, Price, we can't fucking stop here,' he said.

I said, 'I don't want to make a mess so tell me what to do?'

VIOLENCE

He said, 'Just open that fucking door and go on the fucking step and spew out.'

I could feel it coming up. I said, 'On my mother's life, once I do that it fucking seals it and that is that.'

I fucking spewed all over the place and then they took me to the nick. They trusted me when I gave my word. I could easily have done a runner, but even though I was a man of violence my word is my bond.

CHAPTER 9

BANGED UP

When I was in Swansea Prison, old Griff, old big Jones and Mr Hayes were good to me. There were some good screws there. I had a job working on the outside party, which means you were passed to do work outside of the prison walls, but under the supervision of a prison officer.

The bells went this day and there was a silence because they had this big old fellow; he was like a biker, he had a big fucking beard and he was a big scruffy bastard. He wouldn't do any of the jobs he was given. If the screws said, 'I want you to clean your cell out,' he would just tell them to 'Fuck off!' We were up in these cells in the prison itself and we were shifting some stuff out to make room for a bed and everything and it was chock-a-block with old chairs and beds and whatever.

I wanted it done because I was going to the gym every afternoon. The screw said, 'Get the job done and get these fuckers working for you and you're off to the gym.' He was happy and everyone else was happy, and I was certainly happy.

I said to the bearded biker, 'Move your fucking arse and carry some stuff out!'

He was just stood there looking and he said, 'Fuck off!'

I wasn't going to miss my gym, so I kicked off and I had him on the floor and I was strangling him.

I said, 'You fucking bearded big bastard.'

He was a big Hells Angel; he had a dirty big head and a fucking beard to go with it. Both of his eyes were cut and I couldn't fucking stop myself. So the next thing, I was dragged off him by a screw. 'For fuck sake, Price,' they said, 'what's the matter with you?'

I said, 'The lazy bastard will not do as he's told.'

The screw didn't nick me. I could have done something I would regret. Anyway, I got away with it. He could have booked me and blocked my family from visiting me or anything, but he didn't!

I remember another time in prison, after I was given the nine months for the Chinese takeaway affray. I didn't fucking mind Strangeways at all, they gave me a good job; I was sweeper-upper in the shirt-making shop, so I was happy with the job I had. But it wasn't to be so! They put me on a charabanc bus and ghosted me out of the place. Well, I thought I'd never have another job like that. I'd been on good money with them fuckers up there. A few extra pence when you're behind bars can make all the difference between being content and being depressed.

When we were on the bus, all of us cons were chained together. I was chained up, cuffed up to this fucking fellow, Crazy Horse, who was doing four years for GBH – Johnny Baker was his name, from Liverpool he was. He had time for me and I had time for him. We used to work out in the prison gym together and all that. Anyway, Johnny Baker, the Crazy Horse, he stopped me from doing extra time. I lost my head with one fucker in there. I went to belt this other con and he grabbed my belt and said 'Fuck you' in my ear.

I was on the cleaning gang then, but I've forgotten now which wing I was on and I eventually became the No. 1 kitchen man. Being the No. 1 gave me extra privileges over and beyond most other cons, except for Red Bands. I wasn't one of those brown-nose Red Bands, but I knew how to do my time the right way. There are two ways to do your time, the easy way and the hard way. The hard way is to make a nuisance of yourself and lose time after time. That way you get to play with the cockroaches in the segregation unit. The easy way is to keep your nose clean and get out of there as fast as you can.

Usually, such posts as No. 1 cleaner were given to those cons that could apply themselves to keeping some sort of order amongst their fellow cons. I mean, you don't want cons wasting prison officers' time in bringing charges for con fighting against con. You had to sort it out amongst yourselves; that was the best way.

I made sure that my fellow cons didn't get into deep trouble that they would eventually regret, and they looked up to me for that. There's always a daddy on each of the wings and it is this person's responsibility to make sure cons are not getting themselves into trouble and losing time over stupid things. I believe prisons now have specially trained cons called 'listeners' who other cons can tell their troubles to.

You're not looking out for the screws, just making sure that your fellow cons don't get extra time. The screws, in return for this, would give me some extra privileges.

There were fellow cons from Sheffield, now they were the boys that were working with me. I was getting along quite well there. I was happy doing my time and everyone was happy.

This big dark lad, he turned your eye, you know, and he was with me on the bus, and he looked a bit like Cassius Clay, a big fucker. That's why you had to look at him twice. He was a mixed-race bloke. They were processing us and going through the leaders and I then became the No. 1 Pantry Man on the wing.

This day, I had trouble with the taps in the kitchen. This Scots fellow, a con, came down; the screws must have gone off the top landing, so he walked into my kitchen and he was helping the plumbers. Didn't he go and walk all over my clean floor, which wasn't quite dry! His big boot marks left a trail and I was fucking fuming!

I said to the con, 'Even my own boys wouldn't walk across here,' but in all fairness he didn't know and he didn't fucking care.

So he walked across my floor and I said, 'Look at the fucking footmarks, fuck me!'

'Don't worry, Taffy, I'll see you later about this,' he said to me.

I said, 'You'll fucking see me now, you cunt!'

As we got to the steps, I said, 'Let's get it over with.'

I hit him with a left hook and he went sideways and, as he was trying to get up, I grappled with him and stuck his head down the shithouse pan. It went straight through the back window and the fucking door and straight through the shithouse.

The panic bells had rung. One of the screws must have seen him and me going in and heard the uproar! The next thing, he had the MUFTI (Minimum Use of Force & Tactical Intervention) squad down and they got hold of me and snatched me off this con and rolled me up good and proper. Of course, I was worried about losing my No. 1's job. I had become accustomed to getting jars of jam, and good food for free.

The boy and me, we were segregated into different cells and you have to go before a governor for your punishment to be dished out. The block was in my wing and, before I was taken to the governor on adjudication, one of my boys brought me tea and a bun. Prison buns are sticky – we used to have bun fights. The next morning, the steward told me, 'This lad you had the fight with has been in before the governor on adjudication and said to him that it was his fault, Price.'

Now when you're in prison it isn't the done thing to grass on a fellow con and I wasn't going to change my ways. I went in and said, 'Sir, it was my fault. I started it. It was just one of those days, I apologise for any inconvenience.'

We were each given three days in the seg unit, the block, but we were still allowed to keep our jobs for when we were released. So that was it. Magic.

I think they were worried about me and this con meeting up again, so it was written on my door not to allow me to mix with the con in cell No. 3 and on his cell door was written 'No. 3 cell not to mix with No. 11 cell', my cell.

Then exercise was given to us at different times in order to keep us apart. I didn't mind being on my own. The thing is, what's gone has gone so it was just a bad old day.

The governor told me that our jobs were safe after we were released from the seg unit. I didn't want to lose the fiddles I had going. After a bit of negotiating between the screws and us, they got me to agree not to do the same again to this con.

I said, 'Leave the fucker out. Fuck me, we're not going to fucking go at it like before, you know. I'm certainly not.'

The screws said to me, 'He feels the same way as you, Price.'

I said, 'He can use himself, I'm not fucking going to start anything. As far as I'm concerned it's all in the fucking past.' And he said to the screws that he felt the same way.

'Right,' one of the screws said, 'leave them both together.'

After all of that, we became good friends, we had a laugh and this and that.

'Fuck me,' he said, 'I wish I'd known what you'd be like,' and we all had a good laugh. I didn't see him again after leaving prison, though.

I was still in Preston Prison: I heard that there was a difficult fellow down the block; the main kitchen feeds the cons in the block. The main kitchen takes the food down for them. There was this one con down there, he had scalded some of the cons that had taken the urns for the tea, because he tipped the teapot over them! This wasn't the prison staff he was doing it to, but to his fellow cons, orderlies just doing a job!

The fellow in the cell, in the block, was the big fellow that I had seen on the bus: the Cassius Clay look-alike. He did look remarkably like Cassius Clay. They sent for me from the prison warders' office, known as the Wendy House, on the tools.

The screw said, 'Come in, Price, we've got a white-collar job for you. I want you to feed this fellow in the block because the main kitchen refuses to serve him.'

I said, 'Is that the one that's in our team?'

He said, 'Yes, that's the one. The gaffer in the main kitchen is acting petty; they are refusing to feed him. Look, you go and feed him and I'll give you six screws as a guard.'

I said, 'What for?'

He said, 'He's acting up pretty violently, you know!'

'Look, you might make a fucking fool of someone, but you're not making me look like an arsehole. I'm going to feed the man, he needs feeding because he hasn't eaten for fucking three days, see. I'll feed him, but you put the normal fucking two screws on, I don't want fucking extra screws with me otherwise you'll make me look a right fucking arsehole. You could pop me down the fucking block with him if you're going to do that,' I said.

He said, 'If that's the way you fucking want it, Price, the two screws, the two normal screws that open the doors, then that's the way you can have it.'

So we went down and Arthur made the tea for him and he had food on a tray. I said, 'Open the door, the man's got to eat.'

When he opened the door, Cassius Clay, he went like this, 'Wahhh!!!' The two screws, they jumped, one went fucking one way and the other went the other way. I was laughing and Cassius Clay looked at me and winked! He knew me, he fucking knew me all right! He was in for drugs, trafficking drugs or something like that.

Then, the next day, he set his cell alight and they couldn't do fuck all with him and had to ghost him back to Strangeways Prison. They took him away, and I've never heard of him after that. I would have fed him anyway because you have to be fair with every fucker; somebody had to feed him so it may as well have been me.

After spending time in prison, I never thought I would actually be keen on being locked up again, but this one time I actually wanted to be locked up! I landed up at the police station one night after having a domestic row; I didn't know where else to go and it was fucking brass-monkey cold.

I had all my things in the boot of my car. It was in the early hours of the morning and I went down to the police station and up to the front desk.

They said, 'What can we do for you, Pricey?'

'Can you lock me up for the night? I can't sleep in the car; it's frozen inside and out and I'm bastard perished; I'm not as young as I used to be,' I said.

The policeman said, 'We couldn't lock you up, Price, as you haven't done anything wrong. You haven't done anything, like.'

I said, 'What if I gave you a little slap?'

He said, 'You're fucking serious!'

I said, 'Dead serious.'

So he said, 'Take him to the cells and lock him up.'

The woman I was with at that time had chucked me out. I had the option of sleeping in the car and freezing my balls off or go down the police station. I didn't want to wake anyone up; it was a bad night. So I went down to the police station and they locked me up for the night. Funny really, because, with my sense of humour, I woke all the fuckers up in the police cells and they were screaming to get out and I was screaming to get in!

I've had my fair share of run-ins with the police, but I'm not anti-police. Policemen like Graham Miles and Keith Williams, they were good people, they always talked to you. I've known them since way back.

I used to have a good carry-on with Keith Williams, he was a right character and a hell of a nice fellow. He used to go the RAF club and we had a pint or two in there together at times. I remember one time when I had some boiled duck eggs, they were gorgeous. I saw Keith in uniform, I said, 'Hey, Keith, here, get some duck eggs, they're bluey green.'

Keith said, 'How am I going to carry them?'

I took his helmet off his head and said, 'Here, put them in your helmet.'

With that, Keith had to walk around with half a dozen duck eggs in his helmet! Keith invited me to his wedding, but I had to turn him down because I didn't want to downgrade his wedding with my presence. I was a bit emotional over that, probably one of the only times I felt really sad that I couldn't do anything to change my past. This policeman asking me to attend his wedding was a great accolade and I had to let him down.

Graham Miles has been a good friend to me and he was a good boxer as well. He could use himself, as well; another powerful lad who could use his hands. He had a gym going for all of the youngsters. I know his brother Howard as well; we used to be on the weights together. They're really good people, the two of them. But don't get the wrong idea: we didn't socialise the time away talking about criminals, as I'm not into that. I've no interest in career criminals or the underworld. Names meant nothing to me, unless of course the name belonged to a fighter!

CHAPTER 10

CORNER POST

Some of the characters I've mentioned will already be known to some of you, but I thought that a little background on some of the names mentioned in this book would add dimension to their inclusion. As far as possible, from memory, I have added details, but that is not to say that I have accidentally omitted certain details. Therefore, on that basis, I hope you do not take offence if these details, most of which are based on what I recall, are not the definitive career details of all herein. Acknowledgement is given to the website www.johnnyowen.com for some of the boxers' statistics. The statistics only relate to the pro careers of the boxers.

Ernie Arnold – Cardiff, Wales
British Light Heavyweight Champion Commonwealth (British Empire) Light Heavyweight Title

Boxed as a pro for nine years at Light Heavyweight

Professional Career
Fights 53 Won 44 (KOs 20) | Lost 9 | Drawn 0
Fought 1963–1972
See also Eddie Thomas details

Chick Calderwood – Craigneuk, Scotland

British Light Heavyweight Title
Scottish Light Heavyweight Champion
Commonwealth (British Empire) Light Heavyweight
Champion Contender for the World Light Heavyweight
Championship Crown

Born 9 January 1937 Died 12 November 1966
Fought 1957–1966

Professional Career
Fights 54 | Won 44 | Lost 9 | Drawn 1

When he beat Arthur Howard, he won the vacant British Light Heavyweight Title which the great Randolph Turpin had vacated. His last fight was for World Light Heavyweight Title; he fought Jose Torres in San Juan, Puerto Rico and was knocked out in the second round.

Billy Evans – Wales

Featherweight

Professional Career

Fights 4 | Won 1 (KOs 0) | Lost 3 | Drawn 0
Twice failed to win Welsh Featherweight Title to Ginger
Jones on points; both went to round 15!

John Gamble – Merthyr Tydfil, Wales
Middleweight

Professional Career
Fights 5 |Won 4 (KOs 3) | Lost 1 | Drawn 0

Last fight was at the Festival Hall, Melbourne, Australia,
when he fought the German Hans Waschlewski and won
by a TKO (Technical Knockout)

Don James – Dowlais, Wales
Flyweight

Professional Career
Fights 7 | Won 4 (KOs 1) | Lost 3 | Drawn 0

They put me in the ring with Don James when we were
only kids, maybe ten or eleven years of age. Don
proceeded to knock several kinds of shit out of me. Don
was hard and he turned out to be a good boxer, he beat
Walter McGowan from Scotland who later went on to
become world champ. He's big with the ABA and the
Welsh ABA now.

Gerald Jones – Merthyr Tydfil, Wales
Bantamweight

Professional Career

Fights 22 |Won 8 (KOs 3) | Lost 12 | Drawn 2

Gerald Jones actually fought another boxer with exactly the same name. He boxed him four different times; two bouts he won on points, he lost one by being disqualified but the last bout he won by a KO. This other Gerald Jones was from Wigan and had a dismal boxing record of many losses, which isn't surprising when our own Gerald Jones gave him three defeats.

John Joyce

Light Heavyweight

John's pro career seemed to be short lived.

Fights 2 | Won 0 | Lost 2 | Drawn 0

Walter McGowan – Burnbank, Scotland

British, Commonwealth and World Flyweight Champion
British and Commonwealth Bantamweight Champion

Professional Career

Fights 40 | Won 32 (KOs 14) | Lost 7 | Drawn 1

Don't forget, as already pointed out, Don James beat Walter McGowan. Remember, I was put in with Don James when I was ten or eleven years old and he was a lot older than me – he beat some shit out of me that day!

Jim Monaghan – Derry, Ireland

Heavyweight
Fought 1964–1966

Professional Career

Fights 18 | Won 6 | Lost 10 | Drawn 2

I fought big Jim Monaghan twice within 15 days, which is unheard of these days! I was his sixth opponent. Just before he fought me, he lost twice to Carl Gizzi – the first fight was by a disqualification and the second fight on points. He went on to fight Gizzi two more times and lost again, one by a knockout and the other on points.

Peter Nelson – Brixton, England

Heavyweight

Professional Career

Fights 8 | Won 6 (KOs 5) | Lost 2 | Drawn 0

This boxer was the original 'Rocky', and that was his nickname! Although I fought him as an amateur, Peter's records indicate that he fought two pro fights in the USA before turning pro in England in 1961. How did he return to amateur ranks and then turn pro again? Can't work that one out!

Johnny Owen – Merthyr Tydfil, Wales

The Matchstick Man
Welsh, British, Commonwealth & European
Bantamweight Champion

Amateur Career

124 fights, won 106. Represented Wales 17 times, winning 15.

Professional Career
Fights 28 | Won 25 (KOs 10)| Lost 2 | Drawn 1

His hero – Jimmy Wilde

Full name – John Richard Owen

Age started boxing – Eight

Family – Fourth child of eight children

Nicknames – The Bionic Skeleton, The Bionic Bantam
& The Matchstick Man

Record – First Welsh boxer in 64 years to win the
British Bantamweight Title

Cause of death – It was revealed after his death that he
had an abnormally thin skull

First pro bout – 30 September 1976 defeated the No. 3
contender for the British Bantamweight Title, George
Sutton, of Cardiff

Website – www.johnnyowen.com

This was the only boxing do I've ever been to, and it was
all the old boys from Eddie Thomas's gym. We all got
together on 28 February 2003. I was really concerned
about the outcome. Gerald Jones, a great friend of mine

who has his own boxing gym in Merthyr, and John Gamble were there, we all used to be fighting from the same stable of boxers. Gamble was British ABA Champion. They've been friends of mine since way back. A good friend of mine, Bobby Wilding, who has a big motorbike shop in Merthyr and once sold a motorbike to Tom Jones, gave me a call about the do, too.

The invitation I got was for a boxing night to help raise funds for the Johnny Owen Memorial Fund. The mayor and mayoress of Merthyr, Alan and Sheila Davis, phoned me up to see if I wanted a lift to the do! In the end, it was Bobby Wilding who took us all in his jeep.

I'd been invited to many boxing events in the past, but I never had the courage to attend because I didn't feel worthy enough after losing my boxing licence for all of the trouble I got into outside of the ring. I was always getting phone calls from Gerald Jones and John Gamble asking me to go to these events, but I always said no.

The reason I attended this particular do was because all my old mates from Eddie Thomas's gym would be there. The event was a part-charity do; we also had a sit-down meal. The do was held at Bessemer's down at Dowlais. The idea of going and seeing old friends of mine from years ago spurred me on to attend.

The evening was very enjoyable, but I didn't recognise some of my old friends because it had been that long since I'd seen some of them and I had a shock. There were that many people there, names too numerous to remember them all. I was surprised when we were all asked to pose for photographs, and when people came up to us and asked us to sign autographs. We had a great night. I should have attended the other boxing nights I was invited to, but it was my own fault that I didn't.

We were all lined up and called by name and we all had to walk on stage and the crowd were told what titles we had won from what years. The club was full to bursting – it was a sell-out. They all applauded and I felt good, I really did because I didn't know what the reaction would be when they called my name, but they all gave me great applause like all the rest. I felt proud, I really did.

Johnny Owen was a champion in the making; his proudest moment would have been to win the World Bantamweight Title when he fought the Mexican Lupe Pintor in Los Angeles, USA, at the Olympic Auditorium in 1980.

After nine rounds, Johnny was ahead on points but, in rounds ten and eleven, Pintor's heavier blows started to take their toll on Johnny.

Sadly, winning that title was not to be and his biggest battle had only just begun. In round twelve of the bout on the night of 19 September 1980, Johnny was knocked down by a punch and lapsed into a coma, from which he never regained consciousness. Six weeks later, at the age of 24, he died.

In 2002, an appeal was launched to raise £40,000 to erect a statue in memory of Johnny's fight for Wales. The man who headed the appeal was the man who had carried the Welsh flag into the ring on the night of Johnny's last fight, Graham Walters.

On 2 November 2002, Lupe Pintor was to have unveiled

the statue of Johnny. But, in a fitting tribute to Johnny, he beckoned Dick Owen, Johnny's father, to assist him. The Welsh National Anthem filled Merthyr Tydfil's town centre as the two men carried out the unveiling.

I often have a pint with Johnny's father, a nice guy. Johnny was another good boy from Merthyr. They did the right thing by putting the statue of him alongside that of Howard Winston: both were great men.

Cliff Purnell – Weston-super-Mare
Heavyweight
Fought 1951–1964

Professional Career
Fights 57 | Won 19 | Lost 35 | Drawn 2
This man was also known as the Bath Bombshell. I was his last opponent in his boxing career when I fought him in Ebbw Vale, Wales; I stopped it early when it ended for him in round four by a Technical Knockout. This man was no mug; he had fought the likes of Henry Cooper during his long boxing career.

Roy Seward – Lincoln, England
Middleweight/Heavyweight
Midlands Area Champion

Professional Career
Fights 14 | Won 5 (KOs 5) | Lost 9 | Drawn 0
Looking at Seward's record, it doesn't look much. His career was cut short due to mental illness, but at his best

he was fighting the likes of Jack Bodell. I beat Seward when we fought in Ebbw Vales, Wales.

Eddie Thomas, Merthyr Tydfil, Wales

Welsh, British, Empire & European Welterweight Champion

Born 27 July 1926 Died 1997

Professional Career
Fights 48 |Won 40 (KOs 13) | Lost 6 | Drawn 2
Managed World Champs – Howard Winston (Wales) and Ken Buchanan (Scotland)

Clever corner man – World-renowned cuts man

Businessman – Owned a coalmine!

Nickname – The Merthyr Marvel

Eddie was a huge influence on my life when he took me under his guidance.

Hughie Thomas, Merthyr, Wales

Welsh Bantamweight Champion
Hughie fought Roy Bell at Abergavenny, Wales, for the vacant Welsh Bantamweight title and won by a TKO on 26 May 1952. He fought Hadyn Jones for the Welsh Featherweight Title on 26 October 1953 at Cardiff, and lost on points in a twelve-round fight.

CORNER POST

Steve Walsh – Southport, England

Heavyweight

Nearly got to fight him. This is his record.

Professional Career

Fights 8 | Won 3 (KOs 0) | Lost 5 | Drawn 0

Howard Winstone – Merthyr Tydfil, Wales

British, European and World Featherweight Champion

Commonwealth Games Gold Medal and ABA Bantamweight Champion

Born 15 April 1939 Died 30 September 2000

Professional Career

Fights 67 | Won 61 (KOs 27) | Lost 6 | Drawn 0

Nickname – The Welsh Wizard

Honours – Won a Lonsdale Belt outright

Manager – Eddie Thomas

Longest unbeaten run – 34 fights

Record – Never lost his European title in the ring

Abnormalities – Lost the top of three fingers on his right hand in an accident, yet continued with his career!

Couldn't keep the weight off – Weakened by having to

217

shed weight to make the 9st limit, Winstone lost his world title to Jose Legra in a title defence at Porthcawl, Wales and retired at the age of 29.

I was privileged to have trained and sparred (very lightly) with the Welsh Warrior, Howard Winstone. He hit me seven times before I turned around. He was a much lighter guy, he could hit you, but the impact wouldn't be as hard as a heavyweight could punch, but he was lightning-fast.

Billy Wynter – Antigua and Barbuda
Heavyweight
Fought 1964–1973

Professional Career
Fights 45 | Won 11 | Lost 31 | Drawn 3

I fought this powerful black boxer who had been up against the likes of Cliffy Field, Joe Bugner and Richard Dunn. I won in round five by TKO when I boxed him in Penarth, Wales. Although his stats show that he lost a hell of a lot more fights than he won, he was a tough character and didn't take easy fights, which might explain some of his losses.

CHAPTER 11

EPILOGUE

There's a lot of people in this town and many of them have known me from my childhood. Although there are a lot of good people, there are also people willing to stir shit and make trouble. I can't understand how people can be like that. I'm not a fellow like that, but there's plenty of bad bastards around.

In Merthyr, it's hard to live down your past. There are some evil people that gloat and put people in the shit. I know a fellow called John Dee; he's the most decent fellow you would ever wish to meet. You would never hear that man talk about any other fellow or women in a bad way because he's a perfect gentleman; he keeps himself to himself. You would think that such a man wouldn't attract a bad word, but I've even heard people gossiping about him.

John Dee has probably never been inside a gym in his life, but he can use his fucking hands, I can tell you. When he starts he can't fucking stop, but he takes a lot of starting up. I've heard people and I've gone up to them and said, 'What do you know about John Dee? There's nothing you can say about that man.'

People, I don't understand them. There are people that will spread shit about the people they don't know intimately. There are a lot of people out there that can make a lot of fucking trouble for me in any way they could, I'm telling you. There's a lot of good, but some people are unbelievable and they will go to great measures to try and get you in the shit and they wallow in seeing other people in the shit. They are the people I cannot understand.

Some people would like to get me in the shit too. People keep telling me that I'm a legend in Merthyr and a legend in many other places. But what's a legend? I don't really know what a legend is. I'm not a King Arthur reincarnate either. I might be the equivalent of one of the Round Table, but I'm not King Arthur. I don't think I'm a legend – I was only a fucking fighter and half of what went on wasn't my fault.

My legend is Joe Louis the boxer – the Brown Bomber. When he fought, they reckoned they could hear his fucking screams coming from him out in the match, you know. The mates he had, he should never have made that comeback against Marciano; he was a fucking old man.

Although I've been pretty violent and lived a life of violence, I don't think violence should be shown on TV in front of kids, who can be easily led. I don't agree with the way violence is portrayed. Look at it this way. Thirty years ago, we didn't have so many serial killers and rapists around as we have today, so where's it all coming from? If any child said they wanted to become a Pricey-type figure then my message to them would be: defend yourself at all times, but don't go and look for fights.

The thing is, I knew when I could walk away from fights or when I could say, 'Fuck off,' and I'd walk away, but it's not easy to do. If you can walk away, do it and fucking do it fast. You know, the Lord said to Adam: 'Come forth, come forth,' and he came fifth and won the fucking apple, do you know what I mean? If you can walk away, walk away but it's hard to do.

When I was at my best, I don't think there was many in the country that would fuck around with me, that's how confident I felt. I didn't feel the gun; if anybody had said anything then it would have been, 'Don't fucking miss.' I've had guns pointed at me, and I can tell you that it's not the right place to be standing if someone is really mad at you!

If I could turn back time, I would like to have gone in for ornithology in a big way and to have used what I knew about birds and animals. There's a fellow, Selwyn, comes to the club and he says his son is in charge of this zoo and they send him all the way round the world and he has a job looking for these birds that are almost extinct. Now that to me is enjoying your work.

I didn't think I would like machinery so much, especially when I drove some of the biggest motherfucking earth-moving equipment you could handle. But the thing is, I did enjoy it, because there's no point doing a job without taking pride in it and enjoying it. If I had been given the opportunity to go through the jungles and learn knowledge about the earth itself and nature, that would have been a dream job for me.

There was many that said, 'You don't know where you could have led yourself, Price. You might have climbed the ladder and been somebody fucking posh.' Do you know what I mean?

The daughter of my father's sister, my cousin Jane, had a brilliant job in Broadmoor. She knew them all, she knew the Krays and I believe she also knew Roy Seawood. Peter Sutcliffe, he's there as well. She'd know all them. You know what she said once: 'I'll keep a cell for your Mal,' because she thought I'd go there. Currently, Jane is spending time in Merthyr looking after my uncle Joe; he's a great old fellow. But she never got to see me at Broadmoor!

If I could change worldly things then I'd get rid of all these drugs. The police told me, 'Mal, marked were the days when we used to lock you up. You were no fucking problem, you would even fold your blankets before you went out on a morning.'

When I was living in those flats on the Gurnos Estate, sometimes there were old people living next to me, and there was these fucking druggies upstairs and it took a long time for us to get shot of them. I said to the old people if they ever needed me, 'Just knock on the wall and I'm there.' I feel sorry for the old people now.

EPILOGUE

I'm surprised that there are not any vigilante groups because that's what I thought it would come to, with drug addicts causing an increase in the crime rate. I'll be honest with you, I am prepared to join the fucker, me, if they did form a vigilante group then I would be the first one there to accompany the organisers.

I think the difference between killing and not killing is easy; it only takes an extra two to three seconds in some cases and the fellow could be smutted, you know. I wouldn't want to kill anyone; I'm not that kind of man. I don't want anyone's death on my mind. You hear some people saying, 'I wish him dead ...' but I'm not like that.

People have stood back sometimes when I've lost my head, but I would never turn on a friend, not as such. I've got a friend who I trust with my life and vice versa. I trust Mahoney with my life and Mahoney trusts me with his life.

The self-discipline of boxing played an important part in my life, but how much of a part that played in my life when I was away from boxing, I don't really know. I wasn't that strict on myself. I wasn't living the life of a monk who resisted all temptation. I'm a normal man with normal feelings and I like normal things like any other man does.

I've never had any shortage of women in my life, and neither have any of the boys on the motorways. But, once you meet the one that you want, you stick with them. I didn't class myself as God's gift to women. I didn't think I was as good-looking as anything, no I didn't.

I believe in most men there is a certain amount of

violence. Every man has a bit of fight in him, but some of them have to look deeper within themselves, further than most. The fight is there if you search for it; people don't think they've got it at all, but they have got it, like the weakest fucking crony you could see on earth. If someone broke into the house, I believe he'd fucking have a go rather than having somebody hurt his wife and kids; it would press him to his limits. If he's not going to defend his pitch, he's not worth a cup of cold fucking water.

Dicing with death is one man's cup of tea, but another man's poison. I just didn't fear anything. It hasn't made me more nervous being involved in violence, because they never came back for more. But thank God that era has ended. Yes, I believe all men have a bit of fight in them; some are just more gifted than others.

The pain that violence can inflict can be overshadowed by emotional pain. I think emotional pain takes longer to get over than physical pain. I've been through physical and emotional pain. The worst pain I've suffered was emotional pain when I was parted from a certain person. This was a certain someone I wanted to be with all the time and laugh and be happy with. I think I've found that normality now.

People go on about that farmer Tony Martin who shot the burglar in Norfolk. My friend Alan Barnet had a pub that got broken into and he shot the burglar up the arse and he got sent down for it. It's fucking crazy, isn't it, you know, you have the right to defend your own home, surely?

EPILOGUE

When I was bouncing, I had ways of handling trouble. I'd send the best talkers in first and then the others would be my back-up. You've always got to have back-watchers or you could be hit or stabbed or whatever. I can't be watching behind me and you can't do everything yourself.

Today, these doormen, they wear body armour, armoured gloves, stab-proof vests and all sorts; it's totally changed. Druggies go away, get a gun, return and start shooting at you! Yeah, times are changing fast and there are some nice kids out there and some of them are fucking wild. I can't see it getting better with these drug mugs because they get on them and they can't get off them again. It's getting fucking worse; I can't see it getting better. What do you do, it's either fight them or give in! Well, you can't give in because, fucking hell, do you think the Government have the right to give in? They've got to have stricter laws.

I also believe that animals have as much right to be in this world as us; and it's man who is the reason they are pushed to extinction. They're killing them for their tusks and their horns, these fucking idiots, and they think claws will give them sex appeal and they get all fucking sissy on you.

Big fine-looking cattle, give them time and they'll be extinct. They only want the land; they don't even want the grazers on the land. Everywhere you look: even the birds are on the verge of extinction. It's not only the Dodo you'll only ever see in books. Eventually, it will be some of these animals and birds that are currently around today that you'll only get to see in books and that will be sad for the next generation and the one after that. What are you going to do when there aren't any birds left singing?

As tough and as violent as I was, I was lucky enough to have people who really knew me. My sense of humour is still alive, too. By relating a few incidents that are a bit off the beaten track of violence, it might help you not to get the wrong idea about me, and see a bit more of my lighter side.

I remember the time they put a load of sheep and cows in the box part of a motorscraper I was operating. They had left a box open in Pontypridd and then the sheep used to go into them for shelter. Someone must have chased them into the box and shut the apron, so, when I started to open it after going back to work, the sheep started jumping out of the box. It was crazy seeing all these sheep jumping out from a box capable of holding fifty tons of earth, especially when the machine was being driven at speed!

One time, the boys put a load of cats in my car in Pontypridd. These were wild cats (Red Perils), and they were living on the land along the bottom of the tip there. I had an old car and you could smell the cats for weeks after they had been in it.

By the time I got down to Pontypridd, they were all waiting for me in the pub. They had two pints ready for me. I know who did it; it was McClafety, and he got his glasses and lifted them on to his forehead and he said, 'I don't know anything, Price,' and he had a smirk on his face. I didn't go off it with him and break his jaw. People got up to all sorts of pranks that they played on me and I accepted it all as good humour.

As well as having a sense of humour, I've also got a great sense of loyalty. I sent flowers when big Mike Coleman died up London way. He was living with a piece, and we couldn't make it up there because there was floods everywhere. He died a lonely old bugger! None of his family went to his funeral or nothing, and me and the boys were working. We were told on the Tuesday that the funeral was on the Thursday morning; it was too short notice to get there.

On a Sunday, Mike Coleman used to phone me to say how he was with his back and all that sort of crack; it's a shame that he had to go that way. This woman took him in and he died of cancer. His father, when he was alive, was head of the police in Bridgend. I was in his house when his mam was alive as well, but I remember his father asking me, 'Are you this gentleman who is getting my son into all these problems?'

I said, 'No, sir. No, sir.' Well, you have to have some respect.

He had been locked up before because he pinched buses as well; we've all pinched buses!

Which reminds me, there was a bus outside the station, it was there to pick the kids up from the trip from one of the clubs. I saw the bus standing outside the station and we had nowhere else to go. I didn't know it was for the kids at the time of taking it or I wouldn't have taken that particular bus.

We should really have gone to the pub, but we couldn't get in so we were killing time around the town; waiting for opening time. I spotted old Ken the Post, God loved him; Ken Bevan was his name. He's been to America and all over. He used to work for the local post office but that was a few years ago now.

We took him on the bus with us and he sat on the back seat. I jumped in the saddle and she started up. I said to the rest of the lads, 'Jump on or I'll see you later on,' because they didn't think I was really going to go. One or two jumped on.

'I wouldn't mind,' said Ken the Post, 'going to the seaside.'

I looked at the gauge and it was full of diesel, so I said, 'We'll go for a short spin.' When we got back, we dropped Ken the Post off at a house on Brecon Road, and stopped the bus outside the Park.

'Price,' said old Ken the Post, 'you put ten years on to my life. I feel young again.'

I said, 'OK, Ken, I'll see you again at the Buffalos.' About six months after that he had a stroke and he died. I went into the hospital to visit the old beggar, what a character he had been.

After we had dropped off Ken, I took the bus up as far as the Buffalos pub and left Northy to park it up. We could hear all the police cars, 'Whooooo!' They were all looking for the bus. If that hadn't gone on then I'd have put it beside the station and no one would have known, but with the police cars chasing us, Northy and me, we went down through the alleyway.

EPILOGUE

I'd left the bus, parked up, the brakes were safely on and everything and we were down under the wall and hiding.

I said to Northy, 'Do you think we'll get out of this, Northy?'

Northy said, 'Be quiet, Price!'

There was a policeman leaning on the parapet above us and he said, 'Come on out, you pair of bastards.'

We went into the police station and we were full of booze, but we hadn't even scratched the bus. I was ordered by the court to pay a £250 fine and I lost my licence. So I didn't go unpunished and, into the bargain, I managed to give an ageing man a good time six months before he died. Not that I'm justifying what I did, but I would do it again if it were to bring back old Ken the Post.

Another barmy incident shows another side of me. I was staying down at Liverpool and we were coming back for the weekend; it was a long weekend for me, and I got a second-class return train ticket.

I had bought an old Morris Oxford, which I'd left in Wales. It was blue on the top half and white on the bottom half, two-tone. She was all Morris Oxford – leather seats. She was an old rust box, too, but had a good engine and I gave £35 for her. I bought the car from the father of one of the boys who was working on Seaforth Dock. I came down to see the old girl and all my mates.

There was a dance up in the school or something, so Ginger and me went to this dance and I parked the car up and into the dance we went. When we came out, I saw my car there so jumped in it and I thought, who put this cushion here? It was exactly the same as my car; I didn't know it was someone else's car, did I. Mine was just over from this car. We'd gone to the wrong car, you see, but the keys fitted and everything. So I took the old cushion from behind me and chucked it in the back.

It was Howell Thomas the sergeant's car. He'd known me since I was a kid and he knew my family, my mother and father.

Howell said, 'Get out of the car.'

I said, 'What's wrong? What's happened then?'

He said, 'You've pinched a car.'

I said, 'I've never pinched anything in my life.

I said, 'I'm only down for the weekend, and I'm going back on Monday morning. It's my bastard car!'

'Come here,' he said and we went back into the pound and he said, 'Whose car is that then?'

I looked at it and he said, 'Well, I'll not bother this time, but you can fuck off to wherever you are going to for a long time!'

The keys fitted and everything! Two cars exactly alike!

I've had my fair share of incidents with vehicles, but none more so than the day I was nearly killed in a bad accident. I turned up at the pub on a Sunday and a mate of mine, who's a brickie, was there. He's another big lad and a big drinker, big Nigel Norman. We were drinking together and having a laugh, the normal thing on a Sunday morning and Nigel, feeling full of himself, said, 'Pricey, being a lovely day, I wouldn't mind a run out in the car some place, have a few pints somewhere else and come back here and finish it off.'

I said, 'Where are you thinking about going then?'

He said, 'We could go down to Cardiff.'

'Cardiff's a long old way,' I said.

He suggested a nearby place. 'What about Mountain Ash?'

I agreed. 'I don't mind there, but we've had a few pints and neither of us will be able to drive.'

He said, 'It will have to be a taxi then.'

I said, 'Christ almighty, it'll cost us a bloody fortune! We could have called by to see old Joe Walsh on the way back, an old mate of mine, but not by taxi.'

A little voice come into our conversation: 'I'll take you to wherever you want to go!'

The voice was that of little Benny Evans, a hell of a boy. He looked sober enough to me.

Benny said, 'I've got a van, I'll take you wherever you want to go.'

I said, 'Sound, where's the van?'

He said, 'It's just around the corner.'

I said, 'Are you all right to drive?'

'Aye,' he said.

I got in the front and Nigel got in the back. On the way down, we decided to have a pint in this pub in Quaker's Yard, in Merthyr, so we ended up having two pints and set off for Mountain Ash.

We'd only travelled a few miles; I was leaning over the seat talking to Nigel in the back of the van. The next thing, it all went silent! I didn't know that the van had left the road and it was in mid-air coming down through trees, after hurtling over a 50ft embankment!

I could see these trees coming towards me and I thought we were going through this fucking hedge and I was waiting to end up in somebody's garden in a matter of seconds. But these branches were coming through the window and we were falling downwards. And the next thing, we must have hit the ground!

Afterwards, they reckon the van must have turned over about four times. I felt the bump and I was out like a light! The van had crumpled like a piece of paper, trapping Benny and me in the front. The demolished metal front end was digging into my legs – I was trapped! Benny was trapped underneath me. We had to be cut out. The big fellow, Nigel, kicked the back doors open and got himself out. If the van had gone up in flames then I believe that Benny and me would have died in that van.

What had happened, I found out later, was that Benny had missed this bend and went straight on. We somehow managed to miss a bungalow by about ten yards, but if Benny had gone a few more yards on, we'd have gone through the roof of a bungalow!

When I came around, I was in the hospital. They were stitching me up like an old leather football; I've still got the dent in my thigh where the metal was digging in and my hands had to be stitched up as well.

Benny was breathalysed and found to be over the limit; the court gave him a £700 fine. I was unaware of how much Benny had had to drink, as he seemed in control of himself.

I didn't see my life flash before my eyes, as it happened so fast. There's obviously too much gone on in my life to relive it in a matter of seconds. When I woke up in the hospital, I thought, where am I now? I thank God for our three lives being saved; we went through the branches of the trees, and maybe that saved our fall.

I go through all of that violence in my life and, the next thing, I could have gone out of the world in a flash due to no fault of my own. I do respect what that has taught me about valuing my life. I've thought and thought about that.

That happened in July 2002, but I had an accident in my own car in February 2002 when I went to lead Steve Richards into Merthyr, as he wasn't sure of the way to my house. I set off from my home to where Steve was lost in Merthyr and, bang! He drove into the back of me! I remember Steve felt terrible because he said that if it hadn't been for him then I wouldn't have wrecked my car. Luckily I wasn't injured and the car was repaired quickly. Steve said that I deserved a new car for what he put me through and we all had a good laugh, safe in the knowledge that I wasn't injured.

These near-death experiences have compelled me to look back over my life, and wonder whether I could have done things differently. And all I can come up with is that I cannot erase what has happened; I accept what I have been involved in as being part of my chequered past.

Violence has ceased to be part of my life. I didn't turn my back on it – it turned its back on me. And for that I am thankful. Sometimes, in those immortal words, a man has just got to do what a man's got to do.

Now all that I want to do is to carve out a role for myself in the world of ornithology, which is what I should have done years and years ago. The grip of violence has now gone and left me alone and I now wake up in the morning, and instead of waiting for trouble to knock on the door, I hear the birds singing.

MALCOLM PRICE – PROFILE

Favourite car – Passat

Favourite colour – Sky Blue

Favourite drink – Stella Artois lager

Favourite sports star – Joe Louis

Favourite spectator sport – Kickboxing

Favourite hard man actor – Charles Bronson

Favourite food – Meat, any meat seven days a week

Favourite animal – Siberian Tiger, it's a handsome bastard

Favourite choral song – 'O, for the wings of a dove' by Mendelssohn

Favourite song – Celine Dion's *Titanic* theme tune

Favourite pet – Kim, my German Shepherd, an ever-faithful friend

Pet hates – Small change in my pockets; it weighs my trousers down

Best present – A small pair of binoculars to pursue ornithology

Closest persons to you – A very special lady and my family

Hate – People that have no time for old people (respect)

Three wishes – Health, Happiness and Wealth

Best memory – My mother

Fear – Snakes or spiders

Your hero – Joe Louis, fighter!